The deceptive activist

Brian Martin

Published 2017 by Irene Publishing
Sparsnäs, Sweden
http://www.irenepublishing.com/
irene.publishing@gmail.com

ISBN 978–91–88061–21–8

CONTENTS

1 Introduction *1*

2 Lying and deception in human affairs *5*

3 Deception by authorities *24*

4 Detection *60*

5 Ethics and lying *94*

6 Case studies *109*

7 Lessons *154*

Bibliography *158*

Index *164*

Acknowledgements

Some time ago, I wrote a paper about political lying. Numerous journals rejected it and years passed before it was finally accepted.[1] I thank the many referees along the way who offered comments and suggested references.

For years I have been presenting extracts from work in progress to members of the high-output writing group at the University of Wollongong. For their helpful textual comments, I thank Paula Arvela, Anu Bissoonauth-Bedford, Kathy Flynn, Mim Fox, Xiaoping Gao, Anneleis Humphries, Joe Lester, Michael Matteson, Anne Melano, Anco Peeters, Mark Richardson, Linda Steele, Holly Tootell and Jody Watts.

Nicky Hager, Cynthia Kardell and Dalilah Reuben-Shemia provided useful feedback. Jørgen Johansen and Jason MacLeod provided valuable comments on chapter 6, including suggesting additional case studies. Most of all I thank Sharon Callaghan and Tom Weber who thoroughly scrutinised the entire manuscript and made numerous probing suggestions.

---

1 Brian Martin, "Tactics of political lying: the Iguanas affair," *Journal of Language and Politics,* Vol. 13, No. 4, 2014, pp. 837–856.

1
Introduction

Ron and Sarah are on their way to a meeting of anti-war activists. Somehow, they get onto the topic of lying.

Ron: "Look, I avoid lying as a matter of principle. It's a Gandhian thing. I was very influenced by Rob Burrowes who wrote about this."[1]

Sarah: "Oh yeah? What about this? You're listening to an amateur musical group, and your friend Helen is in the group. You think it sounds terrible, but then Helen comes up to you afterwards and asks 'Did you like it?' Are you going to tell her what you really think?"

Ron: "I'd try to be honest, but in a polite way. Maybe something like 'It was good to see you enjoying yourself, Helen'."

Sarah: "Isn't that a cop-out? You didn't really say what you were thinking. Isn't it *deception*?"

Ron: "Well, I wouldn't tell a lie. I didn't say anything actually false."

Sarah: "Let's try this scenario. You're living in occupied France during World War II. The Nazis come to your door and ask whether there are any Jews in the house."

Ron: "Really? The Nazi argument?"

---

[1] Robert J. Burrowes, *The Strategy of Nonviolence Defense: A Gandhian Perspective* (Albany, NY: State University of New York Press, 1996), p. 183. See chapter 5 for a discussion.

Sarah: "Just answer. Would you lie to the Nazis to save a Jew?"

Ron: "How about this? I respond, 'You'll need to go elsewhere if you want to find Jews'."

Sarah: "But you're *deceiving* the Nazis. You're not telling the full truth."

Ron: "It's only hypothetical. In real-life situations, I always try to be honest."

Ron and Sarah arrive at the meeting. It's a group of eight experienced campaigners, and they are planning a protest at an arms factory. The idea is to inform the police about impending civil disobedience, but only after getting into position.

Sarah, being provocative: "Don't you think we should tell the police *everything* in advance?"

Sam: "But then we'd never get into position for the action. They'd stop us."

Chris: "That's right. We should only tell them what they need to know. Especially that we won't be doing anything violent."

Ron (taking the bait): "Yes, Sarah, I know I said I avoid lying as a matter of principle. But we won't be lying."

Sarah: "So why not invite the police along to our meeting?"

Sam: "Enough, enough! Let's get this sorted out and then we can have the philosophical discussion about Gandhi and honesty."

Who — Sarah, Ron or Sam — is being sensible and who is being principled? The group could have continued discussing lying. If so, would their conclusion depend on basic principles, or would it depend on the circumstances, for example what the police might do?

Truth and lying are important issues in activism, as they are in everyday life. Most people think telling the truth is important, and can get angry at obvious political lying. Yet most parents train their children to lie. Sue is having a party for her fifth birthday and aunt Ellen is coming to visit. Sue's parents warn her to say thank you and tell how much she likes aunt Ellen's gift, even if it is really ugly and unwelcome.

Activism and lying

Ron and Sarah are activists: they want to change the world for the better and they, like nearly everyone who tries to change the world, believe they are ethical. Ron and Sarah are a special sort of ethical activist: they want to use methods that reflect their goals. They want a more peaceful world so, unlike militaries and terrorists, they use peaceful methods.

A complication arises when it comes to deception. Ron and Sarah, without even thinking carefully about it, prefer a world that is more open and honest. After all, too much harm is caused by powerful groups using secrecy and lies to serve their interests. Ron in particular has taken to heart the idea that lying is wrong, but Sarah, with her questions, points to some complications. Sarah's scenarios suggest that being open and honest might not always be a good idea, even for a highly ethical activist.

My aim in this book is to highlight the tensions around activism, openness and honesty. This involves presenting some background information about deception and lying. Chapter 2 covers basic concepts and findings, including types of lies and how common they are. Chapter 3 takes up the big topic of lies by authorities, such as government leaders. Chapter 4 is about methods of detecting deception. Chapter 5 is about ethical dimensions concerning lying and telling the truth. Chapter 6 presents a range of scenarios in which activists need to confront issues of secrecy and honesty, and offers some criteria for assessing the use of deception. Chapter 7 summarises some key points. At the end there's an annotated bibliography of books I think are especially worthwhile. These provide documentation and you will find in them additional references that support the general statements I make about deception.

It would be nice to be able to point to some easy answers, but unfortunately there aren't any. Furthermore, even just getting into the topic can be uncomfortable, because popular ideas about lying, especially about how bad it is, clash with evidence about the positive functions of lying. This clash is especially acute for activists who see themselves as behaving ethically, yet assume deception is unethical. Rather than sweeping the tensions under the carpet, it may be better to start talking about deception and about when it can serve worthwhile purposes.

2
Lying and deception in human affairs

Key points
- Lying includes telling falsehoods and withholding truths.
- Lies can be beneficial or harmful or somewhere in between.
- Most people lie more frequently than they realise.
- Secrecy and lying are often connected.
- Self-deception is common, and is linked to deceiving others.
- Social systems are built on "basic lies" about the way the world works.

Most people think lying is saying something they know is false. Instead of telling the truth, they say something else. For example, a government spokesperson says, "We have conclusive evidence that Iraq has weapons of mass destruction," even though the evidence is sketchy. But what about the more cautious statement, "There is evidence that Iraq has weapons of mass destruction"? This claim is safer: there might well be *some* evidence of WMDs, even though this evidence is weak and questionable. Is it a lie?

A lot of people think that withholding the truth — not saying something you know is true — doesn't count as a lie. According to this view, saying "There is evidence that Iraq has weapons of mass destruction" isn't a lie.

However, it is definitely deceptive: relevant information is omitted, for example that the evidence is testimony from an unreliable informant.

Because of this common approach to the idea of lying, government officials often go through contortions to say things that aren't technically false, but leave out vital information necessary to understand the truth. To talk about lying of this nature, there are two main options. The first is to set aside the word "lie" and instead refer to deception. The other option is to define "lie" differently, so as to include withholding the truth.

The second option is adopted by Paul Ekman, one of the most prominent writers about lying. He defines a lie as "a deliberate choice to mislead a target without giving any notification of the intent to do so."[1] Note his use of the word "mislead." This can be done by telling a falsehood *or* by withholding the truth. Using Ekman's definition, the government spokesperson is lying about WMDs — or at least someone involved in preparing the statement is lying.

> "Lying is done with words, and also with silence." — Adrienne Rich, *Women and Honor: Some Notes on Lying*

For most people, these options are familiar in everyday life. Someone invites you to a party and you decline, saying "Sorry, I have a prior engagement." Actually, you dislike the host or just think you'll be bored, but don't

---

1 Paul Ekman, *Telling Lies: Clues to Deceit in the Marketplace, Politics, and Marriage* (New York: Norton, 1985/2009), p. 41.

want to wreck your relationship by being brutally honest. The phrase "brutally honest" is revealing: honesty can be damaging to others or to relationships.

Your partner asks, "How do I look in this outfit?" If you're sensitive, your answer will be attuned to your partner's expectations. If the two of you are used to being "brutally honest" then maybe you can say what you think, but otherwise you might say, "You look great" even though you really think something else. After all, the question "How do I look in this outfit?" often isn't really a sincere request for information: it's meant to solicit a compliment. If someone is really inviting a compliment by using a standard code, then why not give one?

People speak in code all the time, saying things they don't mean literally. In greeting you, a co-worker might say "How are you today?" In Australia, this is a convention, meaning "Hello." So you answer "Fine" rather than "I didn't sleep well last night and now I'm tired and have a headache."[2]

The politeness code is straightforward in everyday interactions, and can also be applied in special circumstances, with positive or negative consequences. You visit your dying friend Chris, who asks "Was it all worthwhile?" or "Have you always loved me?" You might feel compassionate or polite and answer, "Yes, of course." Actually, you know Chris did some bad things and made a mess of a promising life, and you don't love Chris at all.

---

2 Different cultures have different codes, so in some places this example will not make any sense.

What if your friend, who is seriously ill but doesn't want to recognise it, says "We'll go to the big concert together next week." You could be blunt and say, "You're seriously ill, and really need to have an operation." If you're too polite, you may do a disservice to your friend. In response to the "How do I look?" question, an honest answer, phrased cautiously as "You might look even better in the other outfit," could prevent a fashion disaster.

Codes can become complicated, and not everyone can decipher them. Some people are more literal than others and don't easily pick up on the underlying message. People on the autism spectrum can have special difficulty picking up hidden meanings. This means that speaking in codes in which the literal meaning is false or misleading can provide accurate messages to some but be deceptive for others.

The way people present themselves to others is often misleading. An example is pretending to be confident when you're not. Cosmetic surgery, make-up and holding in your stomach can give a false impression of your age and physical condition. Expensive clothes might suggest you are richer than you actually are.

Social media offer many opportunities for creating an image. By posting attractive photos of yourself, of your travels and your friends, and seldom posting anything suggesting boredom or difficulties, you present a shining picture to the world. Some who know you well may realise they're not receiving a full picture of your life, but nonetheless seeing only the best sides of your friends' lives can be demoralising due to the process of social comparison. It also can encourage a sort of competition in positive self-presentation, which means mutual deception becomes the norm.

Setting aside codes, conventions and presenting a personal image, most people are regularly deceptive in more obvious ways, and not just about telling little kids that Santa Claus is coming. After a man beats his wife and the neighbours call the police, he tells them they were just having a loud argument. His wife, afraid of him, also lies to the police. Both of them lie to their neighbours, either by telling falsehoods or withholding the truth.

Serious deceptions often lead to a whole string of lies. A man has a gambling habit but is too ashamed to tell his partner or his friends. He hides his addiction through a series of lies about where he spends his time, who he meets, where the money goes, and a host of other things. As well as gambling, there are many possible scenarios for a life filled with lies: alcoholism, sexual affairs, theft, sexual harassment, paedophilia, and various diseases.

Any activity linked to shame can lead to deception. If you suffer panic attacks or have compulsive behaviours, you may feel ashamed to admit it. You might say you'd rather not take a flight and not admit to a fear of flying. In a classroom, the teacher asks, "Does everyone understand?" The children remain silent because none of them wants to reveal their ignorance. The same thing happens to adults. The boss asks for feedback about any possible problems with a new policy, and no one in the room is willing to point out an obvious flaw because they are afraid of the boss's reaction. They are all being deceptive about what they think. According to Ekman's definition, they are all lying.

Researchers say that most people are seriously deceptive — telling falsehoods and withholding the truth — on a regular basis, typically several times daily, depending on how this is measured. If uses of conventional codes such as saying "Fine" when you're feeling not so well are included, this adds greatly to the total. Most people think of themselves as honest, but the reality is quite different.

Anyone who has ever hoped their parents would die or wished calamity on their co-workers is unwise to express these thoughts. Someone who always tells the truth and withholds nothing is likely to end up losing all their friends.

Is it a lie?
Going back to Ekman's definition of a lie — "a deliberate choice to mislead a target without giving any notification of the intent to do so" — it is useful to note that some forms of deception are not lies. A novelist creates a fictional story that, in many instances, is intended to capture truths about the human condition, but is not intended to be the literal truth. By being categorised as fiction, the novelist has, in Ekman's terms, given notification of the intent to mislead the reader. The same applies to films. Of course there are some grey areas. Documentary films are intended to be truthful, but there are creative adaptations of true stories that mix truth and fiction. A filmmaker might add the disclaimer "based on a true story," which signals that some facts have been changed for dramatic purposes. A different disclaimer, "inspired by a true story," suggests a looser connection with the facts.

> "Writing fiction is the act of weaving a series of lies to arrive at a greater truth." — Khaled Hosseini

Professional wrestling is a type of performance art, not intended to be a true competitive sport. Is it a lie? Some audience members believe the contest is real rather than staged, so for them a professional wrestling event is a lie, but for others, who know how it operates, there is no deception.

There's another complication implicit in the definition: a lie is "a deliberate choice" by the liar. Sometimes people are deluded. If Fred believes he is a famous author, then when he tells others about his accomplishments he is not lying, because he believes what he says. In many cases, people start off lying and then, having repeated the lie many times, start to believe it. There is lots of evidence that people can come to believe things that never happened.[3] In cases of "recovered memory," an adult may remember being sexually abused as a child. In some cases, these memories reflect actual abuse, but in others false memories are encouraged by therapists, rehearsed repeatedly and eventually felt to be just as real as actual memories. In such a case, a false recovered memory is not a lie, because the adult fully believes it is true.

An important point here — obvious but worth stating — is that just because someone believes something does

---

[3] A highly cited study is Henry L. Roediger III and Kathleen B. McDermott, "Creating false memories: remembering words not presented in lists," *Journal of Experimental Psychology: Learning, Memory, and Cognition,* Vol. 21, No. 4, 1995, pp. 803–814.

not make it true. You may be honest, but that's not a guarantee that everything you say is true.

Types of lies
Lies can be classified in various ways. A simple distinction is between benign and malign lies. Benign lies are intended to be beneficial to the target, for example when you tell a friend they're doing well on a task to give them encouragement to keep trying. Malign lies are harmful to the target, such as when you blame someone else for your own mistake or crime.

> "A truth that's told with bad intent
> Beats all the lies you can invent."
> — William Blake, *Auguries of Innocence*

The distinction between benign and malign lies, basically between good and bad lies, is convenient as an initial classification, but it doesn't capture many of the complexities of deception. A more elaborate system uses colours to signify the significance of the lie.[4]

White lies are ones that seem harmless, and may help smooth social relationships. These lies seldom hurt anyone, and provide no special benefit or protection for the liar. Examples are falsely saying "Very much" when asked "Did you enjoy the party?" and saying "Yum" when eating your friend's somewhat unappetising meal.

---

4 I draw here on the framework presented by Mahzarin R. Banaji and Anthony G. Greenwald, *Blindspot: Hidden Biases of Good People* (New York: Delacorte Press, 2013), pp. 21ff.

Gray lies are more ambiguous in terms of protecting a person by hiding the truth. You've been dreaming about a former relationship and then, when asked by your current partner, "What were you moaning about?" say "Was I moaning? I don't remember." Denial can be more pointed, when someone astutely labels your behaviour. For example, you've been complaining at length to a friend about your neighbour's large new house extension. Your friend says, in a pleasant manner, "You're really just envious, aren't you?" You say, "No, not at all," thus denying what you suddenly realise is an unwelcome truth.

Colourless lies involve self-deception (a topic covered in more detail later). Someone who drinks an enormous amount of alcohol may say to the doctor or a friend, "I drink a lot, but I'm not an alcoholic."

Red lies are one that, millennia ago, would have provided an advantage in survival. This might be stealing someone's food and then blaming the theft on an innocent person, or lying to a romantic partner that "We'll be married after I get a divorce." Your business is going bankrupt but you lie to everyone that it's going fine. You spend lavishly on clothes, cars and dinners to impress friends and clients, suggesting that you have a lot more money than you do — actually you can't really afford your luxuries. (Note that lying can occur via deeds as well as words.) Red lies are involved in many types of corruption, as well as threats that will never be carried out: "You'll regret this" or "I'll kill you."

Blue lies are falsehoods intended to convey a deeper truth. You say "I've always loved you" when you believe love is the essence of the relationship even though there were plenty of times without love, or filled with active hate.

Secrecy and lies
Your friend Chris asks you to keep a secret. Chris is planning to leave Sam after many years together, but doesn't want Sam to know about it just yet. You say to Chris, "I won't tell anyone." Depending on who you interact with, you're probably going to have to lie or break your promise. If you see Sam on a daily basis, then you have to withhold the truth. That may be awkward, especially if Sam says, "Things haven't been going well with Chris recently. I'm not sure what to do." This is a plea for sympathy or help, and the challenge of keeping Chris' secret becomes greater. If your loyalty to Chris is greater, you might decide to keep the secret, but you might decide that your concern for Sam's welfare overrides your promise.

Some people just can't keep a secret. If you want everyone to know some piece of gossip, just tell Al, who will tell everyone else, often with embellishments. However, as Al's reputation for gossiping becomes known, acquaintances will never tell Al anything they really want to remain secret.

When you promise to keep a secret and actually do, this is commonly seen as virtuous. It means you can be trusted to keep your word. But, ironically, it also means you have to be a convincing liar, not revealing the truth even under interrogation.

Many jobs have secrecy mandated in specific domains. A lawyer is professionally required to maintain confidentiality regarding meetings with clients, and similar expectations affect teachers, doctors, journalists, clergy and various others. Many government employees have to sign contracts banning them from revealing information gained in the course of their work. In national security, employees have to obtain a security clearance; penalties for violating secrecy requirements can be severe. In all these areas, maintaining secrecy can mean that deceiving others is necessary, even routine.

When others recognise professional obligations, there may be no immediate tension. Seldom does a member of the public approach a doctor and say, "I'd like you to give me information about patient Smith." When there are formal protocols, everything operates smoothly. Nevertheless, professional obligations can lead to moments when deception is required. The doctor might be attending a social function and meet someone for whom a particular piece of patient information would be highly relevant, and would like to say "You really need to know that Smith will probably die soon."

Secrecy can serve valuable social functions as well as protecting criminals and corrupt systems. It is not automatically good or bad. In any case, secrecy is often tied up with deception.

Self-deception
Can you lie to yourself? It sounds contradictory, but that's because people think their "self" is unitary, namely a single whole. If the "self" has different parts, then one part can deceive another.

An example is an alcoholic who doesn't want to admit to the label "alcoholic." One part of the alcoholic's self knows about the problem, and the suitability of the label, but another part, the conscious part, doesn't recognise it.

Lying to others is closely linked to self-deception, indeed lying to others is often necessary to maintain self-deception.[5] A man who beats his wife doesn't want to admit to himself that he acts like a brutal bully; his lies to others about how good a husband he is enable him to maintain his own illusions.

> "We lie the loudest when we lie to ourselves." — Eric Hoffer

Many psychologists adopt the model of humans having two minds.[6] One is intuitive and automatic, the other rational and reflective. The rational mind is the one we think of as ourself; it is more commonly the conscious mind. Yet many decisions are driven by the intuitive mind, for example the urge to drink alcohol and for a man to lash out at his wife. Amazingly, the two minds operate inde-

---

5 Robert Trivers, *The Folly of Fools: The Logic of Deceit and Self-Deception in Human Life* (New York: Basic Books, 2011).

6 See for example Jonathan St B. T. Evans, *Thinking Twice: Two Minds in One Brain* (Oxford: Oxford University Press, 2010); Daniel Kahneman, *Thinking, Fast and Slow* (New York: Farrar, Straus and Giroux, 2011); Timothy D. Wilson, *Strangers to Ourselves: Discovering the Adaptive Unconscious* (Cambridge, MA: Harvard University Press, 2004).

pendently for the most part: it is difficult or impossible for the rational mind to directly access the intuitive mind. This is apparent when people do things — buy an expensive car, eat junk food — that their rational minds know are unwise.

The divergence between the intuitive and rational minds can be a source of lying and self-deception. Suppose you buy a new phone. You chose the phone because your intuitive mind preferred it, perhaps because of the colour, sleek style or because all your friends are getting the same model. But you don't consciously want to admit to such motivations, so you say to others that you needed all the functions provided or the phone had good consumer ratings or something else that sounds plausible — anything but what you suspect is the truth. And perhaps you don't really know the truth in your conscious mind, because you don't want to admit to yourself that you, like nearly everyone else, are swayed by marketing or social conformity.

Self-deception is common in politics. When politicians lie often enough, they may start believing their lies, in which case they aren't technically lies any longer, but rather falsehoods that are sincerely believed.

At a meeting of activists, Mary accuses Fred of being sexist, because of a comment he made. Fred responds, "I'm sorry if my remark came across as sexist. I didn't mean it." Maybe deep down Fred realises he did mean it, but he lies to save face at a meeting where anti-sexism is the standard line. Or maybe Fred deceives himself, believing he has no sexist thoughts. Mary might also be deceiving herself. Maybe she criticised Fred to get back at him for an earlier slight: she wasn't really concerned about his comment, so in a sense her accusation was premised on a deception — and likely a self-deception — about her real motivation.

This example illustrates the complexities that can arise when self-deception is added to deceptions in social interactions. In most cases, no one is fully aware of what everyone is thinking, including themselves.

Detecting lies
Many people imagine they are good at detecting when others are lying. Employers believe that in a job interview they can tell which applicants are telling the truth about their accomplishments and aptitudes and which ones are giving exaggerated or fabricated accounts. Police believe they can tell when suspects are lying. Parents believe they can tell when their teenage children are lying.

There's research on this, and it shows that these beliefs are usually wrong.[7] Most people, indeed nearly all people, cannot distinguish a lie from the truth just by watching someone or hearing them speak. Their rates of success are little better than flipping a coin.

This is despite various manuals giving advice on detecting lies, for example by noticing that liars give fewer details in their accounts or have more facial tics or

---

7 See Ekman, *Telling Lies*; Gerald R. Miller and James B. Stiff, *Deceptive Communication* (Newbury Park, CA: Sage, 1993); Aldert Vrij, *Detecting Lies and Deceit: Pitfalls and Opportunities,* 2nd edition (Chichester, West Sussex: John Wiley & Sons, 2008). See chapter 4 for more on this.

move their eyes in certain ways.[8] Some of this advice has entered popular culture, but it seems not to have enabled much improvement in lie detection capabilities. Anyone who says they can always detect a lie is simply wrong, though they probably believe they do have this capacity. Indeed, anyone who says they can detect lies most of the time is almost certainly wrong.

The flip side of being poor at detecting lies is that most people can be convincing liars. Paul Ekman carried out revealing experiments in which student nurses watched one of two videos. One video showed a gory medical scene involving burns and an amputation, the other a placid ocean scene. The students believed that hiding their feelings was an important skill for their future careers, and so had a strong incentive to avoid revealing their emotions. Most of them were successful: observers of the students could not determine which video they had watched.[9]

Rather than trying to detect lies by observing a person, it is far more reliable to check facts. If someone says they have a degree from Oxford, then ask to see their diploma or contact the university for verification. When a co-worker says he was ill and couldn't take a shift, you might know he was recovering from a big night on the town — you saw him come home early in the morning and stagger into the house.

---

8 For example, Jo-Ellan Dimitrius and Mark Mazzarella, *Reading People: How to Understand People and Predict their Behavior— Anytime, Anyplace* (New York: Random House, 1998).

9 Ekman, *Telling Lies,* pp. 54–56.

Basic lies

There are some features of society about which there seems to be a conspiracy to ignore or misrepresent: no one speaks the truth, even though everyone knows it. Such features can be called "basic lies."[10] They are related to ideology, which is a set of concepts for understanding the world, serving some groups more than others.

Basic lies can be different in different places. An example is the idea that everyone is equal before the law. Judges and politicians usually support this idea, which is central to maintaining trust in the legal system, even though they know there are serious biases in courts, for example with the rich being treated differently than the poor.[11]

In the media, a basic lie is that journalists can report the news without bias, just by reporting the facts. Most journalists need to maintain this illusion in order to continue their work, otherwise they become propagandists or advertisers. The way that news stories are constructed helps maintain the illusion of objectivity.[12] Did you ever see a news story starting out with a personal approach such as, "I talked to various people and this is what I discovered"?

---

10 F. G. Bailey, *The Prevalence of Deceit* (Ithaca, NY: Cornell University Press, 1991).

11 Adam Benforado, *Unfair: The New Science of Criminal Injustice* (New York: Crown, 2015).

12 Paul H. Weaver, *News and the Culture of Lying* (New York: Free Press, 1994).

In many countries with systems of representative government, most people say they live in a "democracy," which means rule by the people, implying citizens directly make decisions that affect them. In practice, people vote for those who will govern them, something far from the original idea of a democracy in ancient Greece.[13] Elected politicians commonly claim a mandate for some policy or other, when actually being elected does not necessarily mean anyone voted for a particular policy (a referendum would be required for that), and being supported by a majority of voters does not imply that everyone supported the politician.

In many countries, most citizens believe that "we" are the good guys and "they" (some enemy or stigmatised group) are the bad guys. In the US after 9/11, politicians, the media and much of the population believed that the US was an innocent victim of an unprovoked attack: US government policies were seen as benevolent rather than interventionist, self-serving, even imperialistic.[14]

Closer to home is the common belief in some countries about "stranger danger," namely that children are under threat from human predators eager to kidnap or assault them. Research shows that the greatest threat to children is from their own family members (and from

---

13 David Van Reybrouck, *Against Elections: The Case for Democracy* (London: Bodley Head, 2016).

14 Mark Cronlund Anderson, *Holy War: Cowboys, Indians, and 9/11s* (Regina, Saskatchewan: University of Regina Press, 2016); Ziauddin Sardar and Merryl Wyn Davies, *Why Do People Hate America?* (Cambridge: Icon, 2002).

vehicles). Yet this information seems to have little impact on the way people think about danger.

To call something a basic lie implies that people actually realise what is going on but choose to proceed according to the shared illusion. This is like the story of the emperor's new clothes, except that when a child (or a cynic) cries out that the emperor is naked, no one pays attention. For many basic lies, there are critics and challengers who set about exposing them, but this seems to have little impact: most people carry on just the same.

Conclusion
Most people like to think of themselves as honest, and believe honesty is the best personal policy. Therefore it can be a shock to examine the evidence that most people regularly deceive others and themselves. Another common belief is that lying is almost always bad, yet in interpersonal interactions, lying can be beneficial in maintaining relationships and even in helping others.

However, some forms of deception are quite harmful. Lies by authorities often serve the interests of people at the top of organisations at the expense of workers and the community.

The result is that the usual idea that honesty is good and lying is bad needs to be modified, and this makes life more complicated. Truth-telling has a social value to be sure, but it needs to be balanced against other values.

Another complication is that because most people believe lying is always bad, then catching someone in a lie (a political opponent for example) can be a potent method of attack. The most common way to respond to such

Lying and deception in human affairs 23

attacks is to assert one's honesty, and sometimes this involves further deception, for example about what one has said or done. The result is ever more layers of deception.

Reproduced by permission of Polyp, http://polyp.org.uk

3
Deception by authorities

Key points
- Deception by authorities is often more damaging than deception between individuals.
- Powerful groups, to reduce outrage over their actions, use the methods of cover-up, devaluation, reinterpretation, official channels and intimidation, as shown in the cases of Abu Ghraib and the Nazi T4 programme.
- Authorities can deceive through propaganda, infiltration of activist groups, and secrecy.

When authorities engage in deception, it is often a serious matter. The category "authorities" includes politicians, corporate executives, government officials, police commanders, religious leaders, trade union officials, scientific experts and a host of others in positions of power and assumed trust. "Authorities" can include both individuals and the organisations they represent.

Just as with interpersonal lies, deception by authorities is potentially beneficial and potentially harmful. However, unlike the everyday lies that ease social relationships, lies by authorities are seldom so innocent. If a journalist asks "How is the war going?" and a politician answers "Fine," the fact that the war is actually not going so well is not just hiding discomfort but affecting public understanding and debate about matters that affect many human lives.

Another reason to be especially concerned with deception by authorities relates to Lord Acton's famous saying that "Power tends to corrupt, and absolute power corrupts absolutely."[1] Authorities in this context refers to individuals and small groups at the top of hierarchical systems, precisely the individuals and groups most susceptible to the corruptions of power. By being at the apex of a bureaucratic organisation or prestige system, authorities have more power and a greater ability to prevent any adverse reactions due to deceptions that serve their interests.

Activists often have to deal with deception by authorities. For example, many companies lie about the environmental and health effects of their activities. A classic case involved the company Grünenthal that manufactured and sold the morning sickness drug thalidomide. Reports started coming in about peripheral neuritis among pregnant women who took the drug. Grünenthal dismissed these reports, made no attempt to publicise statistics about adverse reactions, and kept the drug on the market. Later, a few doctors noticed that some children of mothers who had taken thalidomide had extreme deformities, and published their observations, eventually leading to the

---

1 For research that supports Acton, see David Kipnis, *The Powerholders* (Chicago: University of Chicago Press, 1976); *Technology and Power* (New York: Springer-Verlag, 1990); Ian Robertson, *The Winner Effect: How Power Affects Your Brain* (London: Bloomsbury, 2012).

drug being withdrawn. Nevertheless, Grünenthal fought against legal claims for many years.

Grüenthal's behaviour involved systematic deceptions at various levels. The company:
- denied all causal connections between thalidomide and peripheral neuritis
- lied to doctors who wrote asking whether the side effect of peripheral neuritis had been seen before
- tried to conceal the number of cases reported to the company
- tried to suppress publication of reports about peripheral neuritis by putting pressure on authors and editors
- sought to counter critical reports with favourable ones by using money, influence and distortion
- ran a smear campaign against a German doctor, Lenz, who tried to expose a link between thalidomide and birth defects.[2]

In this chapter, I give examples of several types of deception by authorities, including propaganda, infiltration, lying by figures of authority, and certain types of secrecy. To ground this treatment, first I present a set of tactics commonly used by powerful groups when they want to reduce public outrage over some action or policy.[3]

---

2 The Insight Team of *The Sunday Times* (Phillip Knightley, Harold Evans, Elaine Potter and Marjorie Wallace), *Suffer the Children: The Story of Thalidomide* (London: André Deutsch, 1979).

3 Brian Martin, *Justice Ignited: The Dynamics of Backfire* (Lanham, MD: Rowman & Littlefield, 2007); "Backfire materials," http://www.bmartin.cc/pubs/backfire.html.

Managing outrage
Today, torture is seen by many people as reprehensible. Therefore, governments do not admit to being involved with it or tolerating it; instead, they lie about it. Let's consider more systematically the tactics used by governments trying to reduce public outrage over their own involvement in torture.

Cover-up The existence of a torture programme, or of individual cases of torture, is hidden from wider audiences. This is deception via secrecy. If cover-up is effective, outsiders have no idea of what is occurring, so overt denials are unnecessary.

At Abu Ghraib prison in Iraq after the US invasion in 2003, guards tortured prisoners in various ways, for example chaining them in stress positions, piling them on top of each other naked, threatening them with dogs and, most famously, attaching electrodes to a prisoner and making him stand on a box. All this was done in secret, with no intention of telling outsiders. Only the prisoners and guards knew what was going on.[4]

Devaluation Typically, the victims of torture are denigrated and demonised, for example by being labelled terrorists, criminals, subversives, heretics or enemies. Devaluation can occur in advance, during or after torture. It helps reduce outrage, because many people are not as concerned about what happens to a devalued person as to a valued one. Torture of a terrorist seems more acceptable than torture of a pacifist.

---

4 For references on this analysis, see Truda Gray and Brian Martin, "Abu Ghraib," in Martin, *Justice Ignited,* pp. 129–141.

Devaluation is a type of misrepresentation. It typically seeks to reduce empathy for victims by using negative stereotypes that do not capture the essence of a person. Furthermore, the labels applied often are false. Political opponents are called terrorists not as a legitimate description but rather as a pejorative label.

At Abu Ghraib, prisoners were called terrorists, insurgents, towel heads and other names. More generally, in the war on terror, opponents are stigmatised as inhuman, evil and dangerous.

Reinterpretation Rather than presenting torture as a violation of human rights and dignity — the normal sort of interpretation — governments use a variety of method to *reinterpret* torture, namely to get people to think of it differently, as less bad. One reinterpretation technique is lying, for example saying that there is no torture occurring, or perhaps that investigations show there has been no torture, when actually there were no investigations.

Lying may sound like cover-up, discussed earlier as a different tactic, and certainly there's a close connection. The distinction is that with cover-up, outsiders don't even know anything is happening. With lying, false statements are made. This is the distinction between lying by omission (cover-up) and overt lying by making false statements. After the Abu Ghraib torture was revealed, one lie was that higher officials were not implicated.

A second reinterpretation technique is minimising the scale or effects of an action. Torture is acknowledged, but the amount of it is stated to be smaller than reality. Also, it might be said not to be all that harmful. The technique of minimising is a type of lying. The US government referred to treatment of prisoners at Abu Ghraib as "abuse," avoiding the word "torture," and the term "abuse" was adopted by most of the US mass media. In this way, the seriousness of the actions was minimised.

A third reinterpretation technique is blaming others rather than the actual perpetrators and responsible officials. Torture might be blamed on rogue operators, corrupt officials, or an out-of-control unit. As noted above, the US government blamed the prison guards for the torture, avoiding placing any responsibility on higher officials. Critics of the government have argued to the contrary that torture at Abu Ghraib was in accordance with policy expectations.

A fourth reinterpretation technique is framing, which means looking at things from a particular angle or perspective, in particular in a way that makes the actions seem more acceptable. Torture is often framed as necessary to obtain information, as a defence against enemies who are plotting to cause harm. In this way, torture is looked at not hurting others but rather as part of a defence against their evil intentions. (According to many experts, torture is not an effective means of extracting valid information. In any case, it is more commonly used for punishment and retribution than for obtaining information.)

Official channels are agencies or processes that are supposed to ensure fairness, honesty and justice. Examples include grievance procedures, ombudsmen, police, auditors and courts. When someone suffers an injustice — they are bullied, cheated, defamed, assaulted or unfairly dismissed — often they will go to an official body in search of protection or restitution. In many cases formal procedures and watchdog agencies do their job well. But when the perpetrator is powerful, perhaps especially when the government is implicated in injustice, official channels may give only an illusion of justice.

When an injustice has the potential of stirring up public outrage, and when perpetrators are powerful, official channels often serve to reduce outrage. Governments may refer matters to an agency, or sometimes even set up a formal inquiry. After the Abu Ghraib torture story became prime-time news, the US government turned to official channels, announcing prosecutions of prison guards involved.

For powerful perpetrators, the advantage of official channels is that they are slow, rely on experts such as lawyers, and deal with technicalities. As processes continue, public outrage declines, reducing the threat to those in positions of power.

The trials of Abu Ghraib prison guards followed this standard pattern. The trials proceeded over many months, moved the issue from the public domain to the procedural domain of the courts, and conveniently targeted low-level participants in the torture, not even addressing high-level politicians and military figures implicated in the system of imprisonment and interrogation. The trials diverted attention away from those with the greatest responsibility.

By shifting attention away from people responsible and by giving a misleading appearance of providing justice, official channels are involved in an elaborate deception of the public. This deception is not a case of lying by individuals (though this can occur along the way), but rather is built into the system of agencies and processes that are tasked with providing justice but are not given the resources or power to tackle high-level abuses. Official channels might be considered to constitute a "basic lie."[5]

To say that official channels are involved in an elaborate deception of the public may be a bit unfair, because part of the problem is that so many people want to believe in official channels. Consider for example the legal system. Many people believe that courts dispense justice. However, those directly involved with lawyers, judges and courts know that courts are supposed to apply the law but justice can be elusive. There are systematic discrepancies in outcomes due to institutionalised bias in police operations (low-level thieves are more likely to be arrested and charged than corrupt business executives), inequalities in money and power (rich individuals can afford expensive legal support), and alarm raised by politicians and the media about certain types of crime (such as terrorism).

Despite these sorts of biases, a large number people look to the legal system to provide justice. They also look to auditors, ombudsmen, anti-corruption bodies, human rights commissions, environmental agencies, politicians and a host of others to be fair and efficient in fixing individual and social problems. Belief in formal channels develops from a young age: children often take things at face value, so if a parent or teacher makes a promise, this

---

5 See chapter 2 and F. G. Bailey, *The Prevalence of Deceit* (Ithaca, NY: Cornell University Press, 1991).

is taken as a truth. Likewise, when politicians make promises, many people give them the benefit of the doubt. As an adult, experience with electoral politics and learning about political lying can lead to cynicism. However, most people have little direct contact with courts, anti-corruption agencies and the like, and so may assume they do what they are supposed to do.

In many cases, governments pass laws or set up agencies to give the appearance of a solution to a problem. Pollution? Set up an environmental watchdog and thereby placate the public. Racial harassment? Pass a law against it. In many cases, the agencies are inadequately funded and the laws are not effectively enforced, and in any case a better approach might be to empower the public rather than rely on a government agency or law.

Belief in official channels can be aided by a more general belief that the world is just.[6] Some people believe implicitly that nearly everything that happens is fair, so they blame women when they are sexually harassed and blame the unemployed for losing their jobs and not finding new ones. A strong belief in a just world often means blaming the victim. It also can lead to undue confidence in official channels.

---

6 See for example Melvin J. Lerner, *The Belief in a Just World: A Fundamental Delusion* (New York: Plenum, 1980); Leo Montada and Melvin J. Lerner, eds., *Responses to Victimizations and Belief in a Just World* (New York: Plenum, 1998); Michael Ross and Dale T. Miller, eds., *The Justice Motive in Everyday Life* (Cambridge: Cambridge University Press, 2002).

Official channels thus are part of a grand deception, not so much through design but through a combination of people's mistaken expectations and beliefs interacting with governments and other powerful groups setting up and pointing to agencies and laws as if they are capable of solving individual and social problems.

Intimidation and rewards Powerful groups, when they are involved in something potentially seen as unjust, may seek to reduce public outrage by intimidating or rewarding people involved, including victims, witnesses, journalists and campaigners. Even the threat of sanctions may be enough to silence those who would otherwise speak out. Intimidation and rewards are not necessarily deceptive in themselves, but they can enable deception.

In the case of torture at Abu Ghraib and other US foreign prisons, it was risky to be a whistleblower: speaking out about torture was hazardous for the person who spoke out. For example, Sergeant Frank "Greg" Ford reported witnessing torture by fellow soldiers. In response, he was forcibly taken out of Iraq on psychiatric grounds, though psychiatrists later said he was completely sane. Other military whistleblowers were treated the same way. On the other hand, there were rewards for those who toed the US government line. US media companies were initially reluctant to break the Abu Ghraib story, valuing their relationship with the US government. Only when another outlet was planning to expose the torture did the reward of breaking a big story outweigh going against the government.

Layers of secrecy
Deception by authorities almost always involves layers of secrecy. To say something is being covered up is to assume that some people really know what's happening: they are not deceived. The torture at Abu Ghraib was known to the prison guard perpetrators, obviously enough, as well as the prisoners. After Joseph Darby obtained two discs with the photos of torture and abuse and submitted them to authorities, knowledge about the events reached a wider circle; this continued as more officials were brought into the investigation. Journalists and editors learned about the torture, but even then it was secret so far as wider audiences were involved. Only after the story became headline news was secrecy fully breached.

Secrecy can be likened to an onion. There are some people, at the core of the onion, who are knowledgeable while outer layers are ignorant. Some secrets remain at the core of the onion whereas others, as in the Abu Ghraib story, eventually reach more and more outer layers. The idea of layers of secrecy is important in any study of deception involving more than a few people. If a friend is stealing from your fridge and keeping it a secret, and no one but the two of you cares about the issue, then it is pointless to talk about layers of secrecy. In contrast, in a major issue of public importance, there can be many layers. Furthermore, knowledge of something being kept secret is not just a matter of yes or no: often there are different levels of understanding, with those at the core usually knowing more — though it is always possible they are mistaken or even deceived.

Media organisations, government officials and activists today know about Abu Ghraib photos that have never been released, and also may know about other torture centres and about high-level responsibility. Much of this information is publicly available in the sense that an assiduous citizen can track much of it down, but nevertheless it remains secret or obscure for most people whose knowledge of the scandal derives from mass media accounts.

The T4 programme
People sometimes imagine that ruthless governments can do anything they like with impunity. One favourite example is the Soviet government under Stalin, responsible for killing millions of people. Another is the German government under Hitler, also responsible for millions of deaths. Yet even such governments cannot get away with anything they please. They commonly use deception to reduce outrage from their murderous policies. Here I'll use the example of the Nazi T4 programme to kill people with disabilities, initiated in Hitler's Germany, and implemented by German doctors. The entire programme was based on secrecy and deception, reducing outrage by using the five methods already outlined.[7]

Cover-up The Nazi T4 programme was initiated in 1939 but was not publicly announced or explained. Quite

---

[7] This case study is drawn from my paper "Euthanasia tactics: patterns of injustice and outrage," *SpringerPlus*, Vol. 2, No. 256, 6 June 2013, http://www.springerplus.com/content/2/1/256. References for all statements are contained in this article.

the contrary: great efforts were made to keep it secret. To run the programme, the obscure agency KdF (Chancellery of the Führer) was chosen because of its small size and low visibility.

Though the programme was classified top secret, many knew about it, notably the doctors involved. They were perpetrators and aided in the cover-up. They hid their actions from those most likely to be disturbed by and to protest against the killings, including relatives, members of the Catholic Church, and foreign populations. After public protest led to the closing of two killing centres, transit institutions were created to add greater secrecy to the process.

Devaluation Under Nazi rule, people with disabilities were commonly labelled "idiots," "crazies" and "cripples." Perpetrators used the expression "life unworthy of life." The eugenics movement, strong in Germany as well as some other countries, devalued anyone deemed to have defective genes. The Nazis produced propaganda films denigrating people with disabilities. For example, the 1936 film *Erbkrank* was intended to justify the compulsory sterilisation of people with intellectual and physical disabilities by portraying them as criminals and subhuman. Devaluation, at a psychological level, also helped enable the killings.

Reinterpretation Language is the most obvious part of reinterpretation: the Nazis used the terms "euthanasia" and "mercy death" to describe the killings, which otherwise would be called murder. Another reinterpretation technique was to rationalise killings by saying that people in institutions were expensive drains on the Nazi state when facilities were needed for injured soldiers.

Outright lying was another standard reinterpretation technique. For example, patients from institutions were transferred to other centres for killing, with guards in white coats in attendance to make it seem like a medically supervised process. Parents were told that their children were being sent to special centres where they would receive better treatment. Relatives were sent death certificates with false information about the cause of death. To disguise the central direction of the programme, physicians and administrators used pseudonyms. Lying can serve as a form of cover-up; it fits within the category of reinterpretation when relatives knew that something had happened — death of a loved one — but were deceived about how and when it occurred.

Official channels The programme was never given legal approval; Hitler refused this because the German people would not support it. Instead, Hitler wrote a letter privately authorising the programme and this letter was used to convince some participants. A formal meeting served to win over sceptical legal professionals.

In August 1941, possibly in response to public criticism (see below), Hitler halted the programme, but this official stop order was deceptive. The "halt" only applied to killing centres and did not apply to children. The killing programme continued, with physicians and nurses outside of the nominated centres killing both children and adults using starvation, tablets and injections, until the end of World War II in 1945.

It was only after the war that official channels, namely courts, were used against the perpetrators. After 1947, the German Federal Republic judiciary mostly made decisions that allowed T4 participants to rejoin German professions, for example by terminating trials, acquitting defendants or giving lenient sentences.

Intimidation Speaking out against Nazi policies was always risky. Parents who refused permission for their children with disabilities to be sent away were threatened with being sent to work camps or having all their children taken into state custody. After Bishop Galen's sermon condemning the T4 programme (discussed later), ordinary Germans found to possess, circulate or discuss the sermon were subject to reprisals including losing jobs, being sent to concentration camps or execution.

The perpetrators of the Nazi T4 programme thus relied on all five types of tactics to reduce outrage — a very strong indication of the potential for popular outrage about the programme. This is exactly what is to be expected using this analysis of tactics: when powerful perpetrators anticipate resistance, they are likely to use a range of tactics that reduce outrage.

What then about challenging the programme? Methods of doing this can be categorised into five types of counter-tactics to the five types of outrage-reduction tactics.

Exposure The key to challenging cover-up is to get information to receptive audiences. Information about the T4 programme gradually leaked out via observations and inferences by relatives and local people. The breakthrough event was a 1941 pastoral letter by Clemens August von

Galen, Catholic bishop of Münster, which was reprinted and widely distributed throughout Germany.

Validation To challenge devaluation, the victims needed to be conceived of as humans with lives worth living. Von Galen, referring to the targets of the T4 programme, said "we are dealing with human beings, with our neighbours, brothers and sisters," describing them positively in terms of vital relationships. (However, von Galen was far less vocal about the value of Jewish lives.)

Reframing To counter techniques of lying, minimising, blaming and framing, the programme had to be named as an injustice, namely killing pure and simple. One asylum director, Heinrich Hermann, used the word "killing" in criticising T4 to visiting euthanasia planners, who were disconcerted by such direct language.

Mobilisation There are two ways to respond to official channels used to give a deceptive appearance of justice. One is to avoid or discredit the official channels. In the long term, discrediting the Nazi regime accomplished this, so much so that virtually any Nazi policy was discredited by association. The other response is to not rely on official channels for redress but instead to mobilise support among the public, for example by talking to individuals, publicising the issues, holding private or public meetings, forming networks and groups, and making public protests.

For many months prior to von Galen's pastoral letter, various individual opponents of T4 — especially church people — wrote letters to or had meetings with government officials, such as in the Ministry of Justice, but this insider approach achieved little. These were significant signs of opposition but they were not so effective as mobilising public support: they essentially relied on an official channel, namely appealing to government officials, that gave only the appearance of offering a solution.

Resistance The counter to intimidation is to continue taking action against the injustice and to expose evidence of intimidation in order to create greater outrage. Those who opposed the euthanasia programme at the time, in word or deed, displayed incredible courage.

In summary, the Nazi T4 programme is an ideal illustration of an injustice in which all the methods of reducing and fostering outrage can be observed. It shows the central role of deception in protecting authorities from popular resistance to their policies.

Political deception in New Zealand
In New Zealand in the years leading up to 2014, a political blogger named Cameron Slater had huge influence. His blog, named Whale Oil, was highly partisan and aggressive, with numerous posts attacking politicians and political initiatives.

One of Slater's specialties was the sexual smear. He would obtain information about a politician's extra-marital affairs and gradually present it over several days. Sometimes he would simply imply that a politician was involved in a sexual scandal, without any evidence: this was the technique of sexual innuendo.

Political blogs present themselves as sources of news and commentary, but are not bound by the expectations and practices common in conventional news media. Slater could present claims and slurs that newspapers would not print but, once online, regular journalists and editors could not resist the easy stories offered. Sometimes Slater fed material directly to mass media journalists, giving them scoops, always in the form of attack politics, targeting a politician or policy proposal. The Whale Oil blog thus served to lower the standard of political discourse in New Zealand.

Slater presented the Whale Oil blog as independent. It pursued a right-wing agenda, but sometimes attacked politicians in the National Party, the right-leaning dominant party. What most people didn't know was that Whale Oil involved a massive deception.

Someone leaked a massive file of Slater's emails and Facebook conversations to Nicky Hager, an investigative writer who was the author of several path-breaking exposés. Hager used the material in the files to write a book titled *Dirty Politics*.[8]

According to Hager, Slater was not an independent blogger. Behind the scenes, he was being fed information from the office of John Key, the prime minister. Furthermore, an employee in the prime minister's office drafted some posts for Whale Oil, attacking the government's opponents. Slater also received information from government minister Judith Collins and from paying clients. For example, a client — a candidate for National Party preselection in a safe seat — paid Slater to take down a

---

8 Nicky Hager, *Dirty Politics: How Attack Politics Is Poisoning New Zealand's Political Environment* (Nelson, New Zealand: Craig Potton, 2014).

political rival. Slater boasted to his friends about being able to tear down front-runners for the selection and boost a wealthy outsider. The key to this was collecting dirt and publishing attacking comments on Whale Oil, while posing as an independent commentator.

The appearance of independence was even more important when running the agenda of the prime minister. John Key presented himself as a positive figure, and didn't want to be implicated in sordid campaigning: that was outsourced to Slater.

Slater, as well as making money from advertising on Whale Oil and from clients, also had a personal agenda, namely pursuing a far-right vision for New Zealand politics. This involved trying to get far-right candidates selected within the National Party, as well as attacking politicians in the Labour Party and other parties on the left.

Slater worked closely with several others, for example Simon Lusk, a strategy consultant for a National Party member of parliament. Several of these allies would send Slater completed articles; Slater would publish them under his own name. This was systematic plagiarism, namely taking the work or ideas of others and presenting them as one's own, and was another form of deception.

Slater had help from inside government bureaucracies. On quite a few occasions, he or his sources would apply for government documents using New Zealand's freedom-of-information legislation, and receive them far more quickly than usual requests. He or his sources somehow knew exactly what to ask for, which was material that could be used to discredit political targets.

Slater would prepare a series of blog posts hinting at exposures, while waiting for documents to arrive. So there was another form of deception concerning misuse of inside information from within government bureaucracies.

Hager in *Dirty Politics* gives exquisite detail about Whale Oil and associated political operations, showing that how attack politics was based on systematic deception. Hager notes that members of the public normally have no way of knowing they are being hoodwinked and that political agendas are being driven by special interests. Hager's book suggests that whenever a political scandal becomes big news, it is wise to be sceptical: it is quite possible that the scandal has been manufactured out of little or nothing, and that it is being driven by players who do not reveal their agendas.

Propaganda
When officials present slanted perspectives, it is sometimes called propaganda. This term gained notoriety by its use in so-called totalitarian regimes, of which the Soviet Union and Nazi Germany are exemplars. George Orwell in his famous novel *1984* offered a chilling portrait of society in which government propaganda dominates public perceptions, in the most stark fashion: the society is involved in continual warfare, but this is called peace, and archives are rewritten so that recorded history conforms to current government dogma.

> "If you tell a big enough lie and tell it frequently enough, it will be believed." — Adolf Hitler

Today, some of these same processes have become standard in countries that are nominally free. Governments employ communication specialists to sell policies to the electorate, using various techniques to make outcomes desired by the government seem worthwhile and to ignore or discredit undesired ones. Public relations is the common term for referring to the work of these specialists, who are also called spin doctors, with spin being the angle or perspective emphasised by the way a message is framed.[9]

Spin doctoring is the government version of advertising, which itself is a pervasive form of propaganda, most commonly on behalf of corporations. Of course advertisements come in all shapes and sizes. A grocer advertising the price of apples and oranges is not being particularly deceptive, even if some other fruits are overpriced and poor quality. It is more relevant to apply the label of propaganda to ads that provide little information while conveying images that appeal to unconscious drives.

Tobacco companies have excelled at propaganda. Those who lived through the era when cigarette ads were freely broadcast on television will remember the associations of smoking with being cool, fresh and healthy.

---

9 For example, Anthony R. Pratkanis and Elliot Aronson, *Age of Propaganda: The Everyday Use and Abuse of Persuasion* (New York: Freeman, 1992); Douglas Rushkoff, *Coercion: The Persuasion Professionals and Why We Listen to What They Say* (London: Little, Brown, 2000); Norman Solomon, *War Made Easy: How Presidents and Pundits Keep Spinning Us to Death* (Hoboken, NJ: Wiley, 2005).

Indeed, it was the genius of cigarette ads to associate smoking with young appealing models, enticing teenagers to smoke in order to be sophisticated and women to smoke to be liberated. These days, in some countries, anti-smoking ads feature pictures of smokers with black lungs and horrific-looking cancers.

Governments and corporations are the major purveyors of slanted messages, but now nearly every organisation has to compete in the information marketplace, presenting a favourable image. This includes churches, trade unions, political parties, doctors, lawyers and environmental organisations. Massaging the message is so standard that it would be shocking for any group to present an honest picture of itself. This would be equivalent to a supermodel or celebrity presented without the usual attention to dress, makeup and facial expression. Paparazzi go in search of candid photos of celebrities, of wider interest precisely because they are unstaged.

Because the word "propaganda" has connotations of conscious deception by authoritarian governments, it may be better to use other expressions to refer to deception by authorities, including image management, spin-doctoring or biased reporting. The apparently neutral term "public relations" has acquired negative associations, being associated with managing a public image by highlighting positives and hiding negatives.

There is actually a continuity between deception by authorities and by individuals. Most people could be said to manage their image in various ways, for example by smiling insincerely, making Facebook posts to create a desired impression, and not revealing ulterior motives.

The problem with deception by authorities is not so much that there is more of it, but that authorities have more power, so their deceptions can be more damaging. If power tends to corrupt, then deception in the service of power is dangerous.

Propaganda, take two
In regular propaganda, an organisation is overt in what it does, for example making statements. The statements may be false or misleading, but at least everyone knows the organisation is making them. This can be called white propaganda.

Then there's black propaganda, in which authorities pretend to be someone else. This method has become more commonplace with the presence on the Internet of "sock puppets," which are people using false names. Let's say there is a discussion of some controversial topic, such as racism or abortion. A sock puppet can enter the discussion and pretend to have extreme views in order to discredit them. For example, an anti-racist campaigner might enter an anti-immigration discussion group and pretend to be a racist with extreme views. This might alienate some of the more moderate members of the group.

Another level of deception is for this sock puppet to take on someone else's identity, for example making posts or sending messages that purport to be legitimate. If you receive an email from me, with my name and email address presented in the usual (or a convincing) way, then you assume I sent it. But it's possible that someone has forged both the message and my email address.

Some spam involves forging identities. You might receive a message purporting to be from a bank asking you to log in to receive a payment, or a message purporting to be from a telecommunications company asking you to log in to fix a problem. Because this sort of deception is so common, relatively few people are tricked; for those who are fooled, the consequences can be serious.

An example of black propaganda is for a government to run a radio station that presents itself as being on the other side, in order to discredit the other side.[10] For example, during the cold war, the CIA ran a radio station from Taiwan falsely presenting itself as the voice of dissidents in mainland China. Black propaganda can involve actions, not just words. One well-documented plan by the CIA in the 1970s was called Operation Northwoods. The idea was to carry out terrorist actions against the US people but make them appear to be carried out by the Cuban government, then led by Fidel Castro and seen as an enemy by the US government. The idea was for this "false flag" operation to trigger outrage against the Castro regime and enable the US military to launch an invasion of Cuba to overthrow the government.

Black propaganda is often hard to prove. Documents about Operation Northwoods became public, but in many cases there are only suspicions and heated debates. One of the allegations against the government of Syria led by al-Assad, engaged in a war against a number of opponents, is

---

10 Lawrence C. Soley and John S. Nichols, *Clandestine Radio Broadcasting: A Study of Revolutionary and Counterrevolutionary Electronic Communication* (New York: Praeger, 1987).

that it has covertly aided Islamic State, nominally one of its enemies, by releasing Islamic militants from prison and not bombing Islamic State positions. The reason for such apparently strange behaviour is that if al-Assad's enemies are seen to be Islamic terrorists, then all the Syrian government's opponents will be discredited, and outside interventions will be targeted at Islamic State, not the Syrian government. Meanwhile, Syrian government forces can concentrate their efforts against its other enemies.[11]

This sounds complicated and conspiratorial, and it is. Black propaganda by its nature is devious. Even when exposed, it is easy to disavow: because of the complications and apparent contradictions, few members of the public will bother to investigate in sufficient depth to determine what is actually happening. Even journalists will be discouraged from doing stories by the time required and the complexity involved.

In between white and black propaganda, there is another category: grey propaganda. This includes cases in which the evidence is not clear or the motivations of participants are hard to determine. Consider the case of the 2003 invasion of Iraq, which was justified by George W. Bush, Dick Cheney and other senior US officials on the basis that Iraqi dictator Saddam Hussein was acquiring weapons of mass destruction and had links with the terrorist group al-Qaeda. Bush and Cheney did everything they could to make the case for war. Were they lying?

---

11 Michael Weiss and Hassan Hassan, *ISIS: Inside the Army of Terror* (New York: Regan Arts, 2015), pp. 144–149 and elsewhere.

Subsequent investigations showed that Saddam Hussein had been telling the truth about not having weapons of mass destruction. Nor was there any good evidence that his resolutely secular regime had any sympathy or connections with al-Qaeda. Bush, Cheney et al. may have wanted to launch an invasion for other reasons, and needed a justification so badly that they believed informants who told them what they wanted to hear but would in other circumstances have been dismissed as flaky. This is an example in which deception and self-deception reinforce each other. It is plausible to argue that Bush and Cheney wanted to believe in pretexts for invasion and ended up believing them, enabling them to be sincere in the way they sold the invasion to the US public.

There are other grey cases. The Tonkin Bay incident in 1964, in which North Vietnamese patrol boats supposedly fired on a US ship, was used by the US administration as a trigger for pushing through a Congressional motion that escalated the Vietnam war. But this might have been a false alarm: the evidence that North Vietnamese patrol boats were present and had actually fired was ambiguous.[12] Cases like this show that authorities can choose to use ambiguity to their advantage, interpreting events and evidence in a way that serves their agendas. This is not a planned black operation, in which the intent is to deceive the public. In grey operations, there can be a combination of deception and self-deception.

---

12 Daniel Ellsberg, *Secrets: A Memoir of Vietnam and the Pentagon Papers* (New York: Viking, 2002).

Infiltration and disruption

Governments and corporations sometimes seek to undermine challengers by infiltration and disruption. In the famous McLibel case, the food corporation McDonald's in the late 1980s hired spies (infiltrators) to attend meetings of London Greenpeace, an anarchist group not linked to Greenpeace International. The group, which had only a handful of activists, at the time was producing a leaflet titled "What's wrong with McDonald's?" giving information about adverse health effects of McDonald's food, poor treatment of McDonald's workers, impacts on the Amazon rainforest by beef production for McDonald's burgers, and other alleged McDonald's shortcomings. The infiltrators collected information about the leaflet, and the company then threatened to sue five London Greenpeace members for libel.

This backfired on McDonald's. Three London Greenpeace members acquiesced, but two — Helen Steel and Dave Morris — defended the legal action, in the process triggering a massive campaign that was a public relations disaster for McDonald's.[13]

The issue here is the deception involved in infiltration. The infiltrators presented themselves as genuinely interested in London Greenpeace's efforts. This sort of deception can lead to distrust and paranoia.

In some ways, just the possibility of infiltration can be damaging to an action group, reducing trust among

---

13 John Vidal, *McLibel* (London: Macmillan, 1997); see also Fiona J. L. Donson, *Legal Intimidation: A SLAPP in the Face of Democracy* (London: Free Association Books, 2000).

members and sometimes creating suspicions about those who are genuine. In some cases, infiltrators develop close personal relationships with regular members, and even have children with them, and are so trusted that when the infiltration is exposed, members refuse to believe it.[14]

Infiltration usually serves to collect information. It can also involve disruption. An infiltrator can pose as an extreme militant, encouraging the use of violent tactics and even helping organise them. The point is to discredit the movement: when the group uses violence, it is easier for the government to justify repressive measures.

In the US government's COINTELPRO programme, which ran from the 1950s to the 1970s, attempts were made to disrupt social movements. One technique was to write fake letters, purporting to be from another activist group, with the intent of encouraging rivalries and distrust. The essence of the programme was to use deceptive methods to undermine trust and promote discord.[15]

Lies by authorities
Police, when arresting or interrogating suspects, may lie as a means of obtaining what they want: acquiescence, admissions, information, confessions. A typical technique is to make threats: "You're going to go to prison, and be

---

14 Eveline Lubbers, *Secret Manoeuvres in the Dark: Corporate and Police Spying on Activists* (London: Pluto Press, 2012).

15 Nelson Blackstock, *Cointelpro: The FBI's Secret War on Political Freedom* (New York: Vintage, 1976); Paul Cowan, Nick Egleson and Nat Hentoff, *State Secrets: Police Surveillance in America* (New York: Holt, Rinehart, and Winston, 1974).

raped." Another sort of lie by police occurs in court, when officers lie about what happened, for example claiming the defendant assaulted them, when actually it was the police who assaulted the defendant. This technique, called verballing, is only sometimes exposed when there are independent witnesses, videos or other contradictory evidence.

To say that police lie is not to paint them as particularly corrupt. In many cases, they lie to achieve what they believe is justice. For example, they may have lots of evidence about a person's criminal behaviour but nothing admissible in court, so lying to obtain a conviction seems justified. Furthermore, many criminals lie routinely, so lying by police is nothing special. The main distinction is the difference in power between police and their targets. When authorities have a lot more power, their lies usually have greater consequences, and there is a greater potential for abuse.

Sometimes police, in search of a murderer, choose the wrong person, intentionally or unintentionally. In intentional cases — which might be motivated by payback against someone they have a grudge against — the police collude to build a case against the person, who is framed and may go to prison for the murder. Lying is central to frame-ups. Months or years down the track, supporters of the innocent person, now in jail, may seek to reopen the case, offering new evidence and pointing to flaws in the prosecution case. Many police, embarrassed by evidence suggesting their own incompetence or complicity, resist any reconsideration. This may not be conscious, but instead be confirmation bias: police interpret every new bit of information in terms of their preconceived ideas.[16]

Clergy are authorities. They do not have legal power to command members of the church, but they have moral authority. In more hierarchical churches, for example the Catholic Church, leaders have enormous authority, with parishioners seeing their priests as agents of God, to be obeyed without question. In this context, when priests sexually abuse children, the interaction of deception and authority is especially toxic. Such priests — only a small minority — carefully select their targets and groom them with gradually escalating requests and actions. The grooming process is itself built on a lie. Then the priest uses various techniques to discourage the child from saying anything about the abuse. The young targets seldom have the emotional maturity to understand what is happening, and join in the deception, not telling anyone, and carrying the burden of a secret for years, decades, even their entire lives. Then there is the deception by church leaders who are informed about the abuse and, instead of expelling the perpetrators from the church and reporting them to the police, transfer them to another parish, where they continue the same behaviours. Sexual abuse in churches thus involves deception at several levels.

---

16 Matthew Syed, *Black Box Thinking: Marginal Gains and the Secrets of High Performance* (London: John Murray, 2016).

Reluctance to release information

Organisational elites seek to control public perceptions. They use public relations strategies to present positive images about the organisation, frame narratives from a favourable angle, and hide or deny negatives. These methods are deceptive separately and in combination. The most visible elements are the presentation of positive images and the use of flattering framing. In the background is hiding of negatives. Perhaps fortunately, hiding information opens organisations to the possibility of exposure and exposés, though these too can be misleading.

In their quest for a positive public image, organisations try to hide what would contradict or otherwise harm such an image. Much of what goes on in organisations is routine and of little interest to anyone, but in most organisations there are secrets that are kept closely under wraps. Those who expose such secrets — whistleblowers, journalists, oversight agencies — are seen as threats.

For most governments, secrecy is standard operating procedure. It took years of campaigning to bring in freedom-of-information laws, and they are often expensive and difficult to use, requiring persistence to obtain crucial secrets.

Most corporations are even more resistant to exposing internal problems, and they can block enquiries by invoking confidentiality, commercial secrecy and privacy concerns. They can also destroy information. Fred Gulson was a tobacco company insider who became a whistleblower, testifying about the company's "document retention policy," which actually was an operation to shred huge volumes of documents about what the company knew about the health hazards of smoking.

Secrecy is one of the primary means by which authorities are able to deceive outsiders.

Governments and protest

After nuclear weapons were built during World War II and huge arsenals created in subsequent decades, threatening global devastation, there has been continual citizen protest, including upsurges of massive opposition. Going by what government spokespeople say, none of this protest has had the slightest impact on official decision-making. However, they are lying.

Lawrence Wittner carried out an exhaustive examination of the worldwide movement against nuclear weapons, including examining records of US government discussions about nuclear weapons development and deployment and about negotiations to control and reduce arsenals. Contrary to their public statements, government leaders were acutely sensitive to protest. Wittner concluded that arsenals expanded when there was little public opposition and were restrained or reduced when the public outcry was greatest.[17]

The lesson from this is to never believe what government leaders say about whether and how they were influenced. Even when they actually understand the impact of protest on their own decisions, they are unlikely to admit it.

---

17 Lawrence S. Wittner, *The Struggle Against the Bomb*, 3 volumes (Stanford, CA: Stanford University Press, 1993–2003).

Deception in science

Scientists are often considered to be authorities, in terms of their expertise rather than their formal position or their ability to control others. Scientific research is a domain in which truth-telling is fundamental to the entire enterprise. If scientists, when writing research papers, intentionally deceived others, science as we know it could hardly exist. If the author of a scientific paper could twist findings, readers would not know whether to trust them. This helps explain why fraud in science — generally taken to refer to altering or manufacturing data — is treated as a major transgression. This sort of scientific fraud can be detected in various ways, including by reports from whistleblowers and by the detection of anomalies in data and methods.

Despite the importance of truth-telling in science, and indeed in scholarship more generally, there are a number of deceptions embedded in publication conventions and the image of science. Consider the scientific paper, typically a concise summary of the research topic, the methods used, the findings and their implications. Scientists know that research papers follow a convention, and do not provide a description of the way research is actually carried out. Chemists do not write "We spilled some chemicals and noticed an unusual colour. So we investigated further and discovered we were looking for the wrong thing." Such honesty about the research process is rare, indeed so rare that a prominent scientist once wrote that the scientific paper is fraudulent.[18] If so, it's only false to outsiders, because scientists know that published papers are telling a story according to a formula.

Another type of deception involves the image of science, the standard picture being that scientists are objective, dispassionate searchers for the truth. The reality, known to most researchers, is that scientists can be highly emotional and in particular highly committed to their ideas, so much so that they often maintain them in the face of contrary evidence.[19] Many top scientists are competitive, seeking to obtain fame via their research, and sometimes engage in bitter disputes over priority for discoveries. Actually, many scientists believe in this storybook image: they think they actually are objective. This is a type of collective self-deception, in which the conventions of science, and the images conveyed in science textbooks, are taken as reality.

The image of the sober, dispassionate scientist — enhanced by the formulaic scientific paper — is useful when researchers make pronouncements: they have more credibility when seen as objective, with subjective elements submerged or disguised. When a government or

---

18 P. B. Medawar, "Is the scientific paper fraudulent? Yes; it misrepresents scientific thought," *Saturday Review*, 1 August 1964, pp. 42–43.

19 Michael J. Mahoney, *Scientist as Subject: The Psychological Imperative* (Cambridge, MA: Ballinger, 1976); Ian I. Mitroff, *The Subjective Side of Science* (Amsterdam: Elsevier, 1974); David Lindsay Watson, *Scientists are Human* (London: Watts & Co., 1938).

company wants to defend its policy or plan, finding some willing scientists can be effective in offering legitimacy. The scientists are presented as objective and contrasted to citizen opponents who are stigmatised as subjective and hence easily dismissed.

There is also another aspect of deception in science: companies may fund research that serves their interests, manipulate results, hide unwelcome findings, and use publications as tools for marketing campaigns. This sort of deception is widespread in biomedical fields, for example in research on pharmaceutical drugs.[20]

To refer to scholarship as a domain for truth-telling is most accurate when vested interests play little role and when researchers have little to gain by exaggerating or distorting their findings, and can easily be exposed when they do. The more general point is that even domains where truth-telling is vital can be plagued by passions, biases and the presence of vested interests. Whenever an area develops a reputation for honesty, it is predictable that interlopers will try to benefit from a false impression that they too are honest.

Conclusion

Types of deception by authorities are mostly similar to those between individuals. There are benign, conventional lies, and there are some major, damaging lies. The main difference is that deceptions by authorities affect a lot

---

20 Peter C. Gøtzsche, *Deadly Medicines and Organised Crime: How Big Pharma Has Corrupted Healthcare* (London: Radcliffe, 2013).

more people and can influence policies and practices with long-term implications.

Anyone who comes up against authorities — that's just about everyone — needs to know about how they can be deceptive, intentionally or otherwise. Protesters need to understand police deceptions; election campaigners need to understand political lying; employees, especially whistleblowers, need to understand lying by managers; soldiers need to understand lying by their commanders; citizens need to understand lying by national leaders.

Despite the importance of understanding lying by authorities, many people give them the benefit of the doubt. They have a "truth bias," assuming authorities are telling the whole truth unless there is convincing evidence to the contrary. Despite politicians repeatedly breaking campaign promises, many voters treat new promises with undue regard.

On the other hand, it is possible to become too cynical, not believing anything a politician or a corporate boss says. This points to the need for reliable methods of detecting lies. This is the topic of the next chapter.

4
Detection

Key points
- Most people can't detect lying through behavioural cues.
- To detect deception, it's useful to assess a speaker's track record, the context and motivations.
- Evidence is often the most powerful tool for detecting deception.

Many people believe they can tell when someone is lying. Parents think they can tell when their children are lying. Police think they can tell when suspects are lying. Bosses think they can tell when subordinates are lying.

How do they know? Sometimes it's an intuitive sense. Other times it's based on specific observations: the other person is looking away, fidgeting, blinking more than normal, or any of a number of other tell-tale signs of body language.

> "It is always the best policy to speak the truth, unless of course you are an exceptionally good liar." — Jerome Jerome, *The Idler*

Researchers have sought to test whether people are any good at detecting lies. As noted in chapter 2, most student nurses can be very good at concealing their emotions and lying about whether they have seen a gory medical video or a pleasant scene. By looking at the student nurses, observers could not tell which video they had seen.¹ This same finding has been replicated many times. The basic result is that lots of people think they can detect lies, but very few can actually do so better than chance. In other words, their lie-detection skills are no better than guessing.

When little children lie, they often give themselves away. Two-year-old Jessica says about her toy duck "I didn't take Freddie" while holding Freddie in her hand.

> "In its natural state, the child tells the literal truth because it is too naive to think of anything else. Blurting out the complete truth is considered adorable in the young, right smack up to the moment that the child says, 'Mommy, is this the fat lady you can't stand?'" — Judith Martin, *Miss Manners' Guide to Rearing Perfect Children* (1985)

But as children get older, they become much better liars. In this, they are often trained by parents and others in their lives. "Be sure to tell grandmother that you really like the present she gave you." "Don't tell your mother I gave this [chocolate] to you." "Tell Sal [who has just called] that I'm not here." Most of these are white lies, told for innocuous social purposes. Others are more serious. "Tell your

---

1 Paul Ekman, *Telling Lies: Clues to Deceit in the Marketplace, Politics, and Marriage* (New York: Norton, 1985/2009), pp. 54–56. For a comprehensive treatment of lie detection, see Aldert Vrij, *Detecting Lies and Deceit: Pitfalls and Opportunities*, 2nd edition (Chichester, West Sussex: John Wiley & Sons, 2008).

mother I'm staying late at work." "Tell the shopkeeper that you put the [stolen] goods in your bag by mistake."

Because parents and other people in a child's life commonly provide training and role models for lying, it is hardly surprising that most children become pretty good at it. The only surprise is that when children get a bit older, so many parents think they can tell when the kids are lying.

There may be a few people who actually are good at detecting lies just by observing someone's body language. Members of the US Secret Service, who scan crowds looking for threats as part of their job, apparently can become skilled at lie-detection, but are still far from perfect, guessing correctly around 64% of the time compared to a bit over 50% for police officers, university students and various other groups.[2]

The conclusion is that few humans are good at detecting lies just through observation, and most do no better than chance. The trap is false confidence, as when police, bosses or parents think they know when someone is telling the truth just by talking to them, or even think they can tell by looking whether someone is honest. It's better to assume you have no clue and thus not rely on observation, but use other methods.

---

2 Paul Ekman and Maureen O'Sullivan, "Who can catch a liar?" *American Psychologist,* Vol. 46, No. 9, September 1991, pp. 913–920. Whether there are individuals with exceptional capabilities to detect deception has been questioned: Charles F. Bond, Jr. and Ahmet Uysal, "On lie detection 'wizards'," *Law and Human Behavior,* Vol. 31, No. 1, February 2007, pp. 109–115.

What about the polygraph, commonly called a lie-detector? This is a machine hooked up to detect a person's physiological signs such as heart rate and blood pressure. The polygraph doesn't detect lies, but instead only the bodily responses that some people have when they lie. If you're calm when you tell the truth but become emotionally aroused when saying something you know is false — your heart races a bit — then a polygraph, with a skilled operator, can detect when you're lying.

However, polygraph tests are not reliable. Some people can lie without a worry, so the polygraph shows nothing different. Psychopaths, who lack a conscience, can do this, and others can train themselves to be calm when lying. Then there are people who are so nervous that when telling the truth on a sensitive matter the polygraph response indicates they are lying. They are so worried by the process that it gives a false positive, namely registering lying when they are telling the truth. Finally, people who have deceived themselves, namely who believe their own lies, will pass a polygraph examination. That's because they think they are telling the truth.

To look more systematically at ways to detect deception, it's useful to classify methods into three main types: assess the speaker, check the evidence, and assess history and context. These are summarised in Table 4.1.

Table 4.1. Methods of detecting deception[3]

1. Assess the speaker
   - use behavioural clues
   - assess the speaker's track record
   - evaluate motives and incentives

2. Uncover and analyse the evidence
   - assess whether the evidence has been a reliable indicator previously
   - expose conflicting claims and statements
   - clarify key points and concepts
   - compare with other views; undertake research
   - test veracity (individually): check facts, obtain statistics
   - test veracity (collectively): get a group together to bring out suppressed information and perspectives; cultivate whistleblowers, leakers, internal sympathisers, investigative journalists
   - self-deception: search for contrary evidence

3. Assess history and context
   - assess past circumstances for their correlation with lying
   - assess incentives for lying provided by the context, for example money or reprisals
   - look at environmental clues concerning deception, for example patterns of collusion or self-interest

---

[3] Adapted from a table in Brian Martin, "Tactics of political lying: the Iguanas affair," *Journal of Language and Politics*, Vol. 13, No. 4, 2014, pp. 837–856, at p. 845.

Assess the speaker

Behavioural clues
As already discussed, most people aren't very good at using behavioural clues, though many people think they are. However, most people have no training in using behavioural clues and have a potential to learn.

Most people are very good at hiding their feelings. When someone says something upsetting, they may mask their feelings of disgust or fear by smiling. However, just before their smile, there may be a very brief expression of their true feeling, called a micro-expression. It is so brief, just a fraction of a second, that it is easy to miss. Through practice, though, it's possible to become better at two things: seeing the micro-expression and correctly interpreting it, for example as disgust or fear.[4]

A fake smile, that feigns the feeling of happiness, is easy to do, but fake smiles are subtly different from genuine smiles, called Duchesne smiles. A fake smile just involves the muscles around the mouth, whereas a Duchesne smile also engages small muscles around the eyes, which is quite hard to do voluntarily, without the accompanying positive feeling.

So if you see Sally smile, through practice you should be able to detect whether there was a preliminary micro-expression, to interpret this micro-expression, and to check whether the smile is fake or genuine. Let's say

---

4 Paul Ekman, *Emotions Revealed: Recognizing Faces and Feelings to Improve Communication and Emotional Life* (New York: Times Books, 2003).

you detect a feeling of fear masked by a fake smile. Does this mean Sally is consciously deceptive? Not necessarily. It might indicate an unconscious fear. It might be useful to know this.

The next question is whether you do anything about your extra insight into Sally's emotions. It might not be a wise idea to ask her whether she's afraid, because this might upset her for no useful purpose. If you don't say anything but keep your information to yourself, now it's you being deceptive! But this is to get ahead of the story. For now, I'm discussing detecting deception; what to do about knowledge of deception is another stage.

Suppose you think Sally is unconsciously hiding a fear resulting from something you've said. But how can you be sure? Even if you're highly skilled at detecting micro-expressions, you can make mistakes. So it's a good idea to check your interpretation of Sally's response. Perhaps you've been talking about putting a protest banner on a high building. Sally might be afraid of heights but not want to show it among activists she respects, and you later observe her avoiding looking down from three floors up. Or perhaps you've been talking about the effects of nuclear war, and Sally is afraid of death. However, that wouldn't be a surprise, because most people are afraid of death. You might learn more about how this is likely to affect Sally by reading about terror management theory[5]

---

5 Jeff Greenberg, Sheldon Solomon, and Tom Pyszczynski, "Terror management theory of self-esteem and cultural worldviews: empirical assessments and conceptual refinements,"

— being reminded about death can affect people's behaviour without them being aware of it — than by trying to observe her response to actual risks of dying.

The implication here is that it may be possible to become much better at reading people's emotions from their face — or their voice or body language — but this may require a fair bit of practice. Furthermore, you need independent information to check your assessment obtained from behavioural clues.

Assess the speaker's track record
If you know that someone has lied repeatedly before, this is an indication they are prone to lying. Some people are called habitual liars: they make up all sorts of stories, about what they own, where they went to school, who they know and what they've done. When caught out in a lie, they blithely switch to another.

Occasionally a well-known figure is exposed for having deceived others for many years. Bruno Bettelheim was a prominent child psychologist and writer whose books were read by many as revealing truths about human behaviour. Then, much later, Richard Pollak wrote a book about Bettelheim, showing that throughout his life he had misrepresented his own past and that many of his research findings were suspect.[6] If, much earlier, someone had made a careful analysis of Bettelheim's claims, Bettelheim

Advances in Experimental Social Psychology, Vol. 29, 1997, pp. 61–139.

6 Richard Pollak, *The Creation of Dr. B: A Biography of Bruno Bettelheim* (New York: Simon and Schuster, 1996).

might not have been taken so seriously. Even so, Pollak's critique offers a warning about being too trusting.

Some politicians make all sorts of promises during election campaigns, and then go back on them after getting into office, using various excuses. These broken promises can almost become predictable.

For decades, the tobacco industry covered up internal knowledge of the harmful effects of smoking. Now that this cover-up has been exposed, this could be a warning not to trust anything tobacco companies say about the health hazards of smoking.

On the other hand, some people have a reputation for being honest, for telling it like it is, for being straight shooters. Some even are known for being honest when no one else has the courage to speak out, for example dissidents in China or Iran. If there is good evidence for a person's reputation for honesty, this is a recommendation for believing them.

However, a lot of care is needed when using this criterion for detecting deceit. A dissident might be courageous in speaking truth in the face of government repression, but still be cautious, only speaking out on carefully chosen times and topics. Furthermore, courage in dissent does not necessarily carry over into honesty in personal dealings. Some prominent figures have secret lives. Whether being selectively honest is a problem depends on your values, and what is at stake.

One problem in relying on a track record is that track records themselves can become a target for attack. To attack a political opponent, campaigners may monitor every statement, finding one instance of an alleged lie (which might just be a mistake), and then trumpet this lie endlessly, seeking to discredit the politician's reputation for honesty. When Julia Gillard was prime minister of Australia, her opponents, led by Tony Abbott, leader of the opposition, relentlessly accused her of lying about an election promise concerning a carbon tax, labelling her Juliar.[7] Gillard lost the next election, and Abbott became prime minister and proceeded to break numerous election promises.

In the midst of all the clamour, it would be difficult to make an assessment of Gillard's and Abbott's track record concerning election promises. Was Gillard especially duplicitous, or were Abbott and company especially ruthless in exaggerating one alleged deception into a long-running slur? Did Abbott really break more election promises than Gillard, and were they more significant? A dispassionate, non-partisan assessment is needed, and this would be extremely difficult given media management strategies by both political parties.

Making an informed judgement about the track record of an individual or organisation is important, yet it is often bypassed because of the truth bias: many people assume others are telling the truth unless there is persuasive evidence to the contrary. If Alpha, a member of your group, has been telling damaging lies for years, this should be taken into account, even though *this time* the topic is different, and there are new members who don't know Alpha and are willing to accept statements at face value.

---

7 Kerry-Anne Walsh, *The Stalking of Julia Gillard* (Sydney: Allen & Unwin, 2013).

The truth bias is especially damaging when dealing with authorities. In court, some police have a long track record of verballing those accused of crimes, namely lying in order to convict them. Judges may know about this but do nothing, even though perjury is a crime. Meanwhile, juries are not told anything about the practice of verballing, much less about the reliability of police witnesses. So the practice continues.

The role of a track record applies to organisations and to social systems. Just because a tobacco company has a new spokesperson does not mean that suddenly the truth will come out. In this case, the pattern of deception is institutionalised. It should be assumed that the pattern will continue. Only if there is a sudden change in the message should the possibility of truth-telling be taken seriously.

The example of a tobacco company is easy to grasp, but the same approach is less commonly applied to governments, at least governments that are considered friendly. Consider the issue of torture. Every government in the world denies engaging in torture. Informed groups, such as Amnesty International, document torture in dozens of countries. So the governments of dozens of countries are involved in systematic deception. Perhaps a government spokesperson is being personally honest in saying there is no torture, because the spokesperson is being deceived by others in the system. The point is that deception is institutionalised, and the honesty of a spokesperson is a related but not essential issue.

For getting at the track record of a corporate sector (like the tobacco industry) or a government, detailed investigation is vital. One of the patterns perceived by political scientists is that left-wing politicians, when elected, often fail to live up to the expectations of their radical supporters, especially when sweeping changes are promised.[8] Some supporters become disillusioned, but the disappointments are infrequent enough that many put their trust in the next great hope. In this case, and in others, historians and political scientists can detect patterns. It is unlikely that left-wing politicians, riding a wave of support, are trying to deceive anyone, but nonetheless many of their supporters are probably being deceived because their expectations are unrealistic.

Evaluate motives and incentives

In some circumstances, people have a greater incentive to lie, and therefore others should be more sceptical of their claims than otherwise. Someone charged with a serious crime has a strong incentive to lie in order to avoid going to prison. A witness to the crime, giving testimony in court, has less reason to lie, at least if the witness is not being bribed or threatened.

If the witness is a close friend or associate of the defendant, then the witness has a motive to lie in support of the defendant. On the other hand, if the witness hates the defendant, or has been harmed by the defendant, the witness has a motive to lie in the other direction, to help convict the defendant. For a witness to be independent thus is important in maintaining credibility.

---

8 Ralph Miliband, *The State in Capitalist Society* (London: Weidenfeld and Nicolson, 1969).

In giving testimony in court, lying is considered so serious that it is a crime itself, called perjury. Yet it happens all the time. Every time a defendant pleads innocent but is found guilty, the implication is that the defendant was lying, yet convicted criminals are almost never charged with perjury.

More generally, a common motive for lying is that telling the truth will cause some harm to the speaker, for example embarrassment, loss of money or relationship damage. Companies involved in illegal dumping of waste are not likely to announce this to the world. Those involved know that revealing the truth will cost the company money, harm the company's reputation, and maybe lead to the loss of their jobs. Criminal prosecution might even be possible.

When talking about the motive for a company to tell lies, there's an important qualification: a company is not an individual, and it can be misleading to say that a company has a motive, because a company does not have a mind.[9] People involved with the company can have different motives. Many employees may not know the truth about the illegal dumping; they do not lie, and have no motive to do so. Indeed, top managers might not know about the dumping. Those who know about it are parties to a deception, and have a strong motive to tell falsehoods about it or at least keep quiet about it. Then there are false

---

9 On the attribution of minds to others, including organisations, see Daniel M. Wegner and Kurt Gray, *The Mind Club: Who Thinks, What Feels, and Why It Matters* (New York: Viking, 2016).

or misleading public statements on behalf of the company, put out by spokespeople, perhaps advised by a public relations firm. The people who write the public statements, put them out and answer questions may or may not know the statements are false or misleading. Inside the company, there can be various levels of understanding, misunderstanding, justification, deception and self-deception, depending on each employee's knowledge, role and psychology.

When outsiders attribute a motive to a company, this is a convenient shorthand for referring to the motives of those most responsible for decisions and/or for public statements. To say the company has a motive to cover up the illegal dumping captures a key psychological and organisational dynamic, but it useful to remember that things inside the company are far more complex. Indeed, it is helpful to remember that any organisation is made up of individuals, so for some purposes it can be misleading to think of the organisation as if it is a person.

Motives are closely connected to incentives. If someone is paying you to keep quiet, the money is an incentive and your motive is financial, at least partly so. Therefore, looking at incentives can be useful for assessing whether someone might be lying. The stronger the incentives to lie, then in most cases the more likely lying will occur.

Consider the situation of lawyers who work in an adversarial legal system such as in the US. In a criminal trial, normally the plaintiff and the defendant are represented by lawyers. In quite a few cases, lawyers know or have a good idea about who is really guilty or innocent.

Nevertheless, it is their role, sometimes very well paid, to argue on behalf of their client.

Many lawyers do whatever they can to help their clients win, for example hammering points of attack, hiding or not alluding to information damaging to their client, objecting to certain questions by the opponent's lawyer, and so forth. In making the best possible case for their clients, most lawyers are being deceptive at some level. After all, their task is partisan, not a neutral quest for the truth. That is supposed to be the role for the judge or jury.

Every role in society contains incentives for some types of truth-telling and some types of deception. Many people think that being a scientist is the perfect role for truth-telling. After all, scientific fraud — manufacturing or altering data — is rightly condemned. Nevertheless, looking more closely, there are incentives within the scientific enterprise that encourage certain types of deception.

Some scientists are employed by companies to undertake research about the company's own products. For example, a pharmaceutical company scientist might test a new drug for safety and efficacy. When studying a drug that shows great promise for being a blockbuster, there is an incentive to show the drug in the best possible light, minimising reporting of adverse side effects and reporting favourable evidence of potency. This can be done in a variety of misleading ways, including looking for adverse effects for a too-short time period, using sample sizes that are too small, using protocols that exclude unwelcome data, and not publishing trials giving results unfavourable to the drug.[10]

These influences also apply to university scientists who are paid by a company to study the company's drugs. So strong is this sort of influence on reported results that it has a special name: the funding effect. Funding is the incentive; the motive for the scientists is to keep the funder happy and thereby maintain jobs or research grants, as well as to publish articles, build a reputation and gain promotions.

So strong is the influence of funding that when seeking to detect deception, it is useful to remember the dictum, "Follow the money." Knowing the source of someone's income and wealth can do a lot to guide assessments of the likelihood of deception. But it is only a likelihood, not a guarantee. There are plenty of pharmaceutical company scientists who do their best to be honest, and some companies set high ethical standards. The funding effect can still occur, because bias can be unconscious. It is also possible that researchers and companies with an incentive to be biased nonetheless produce exemplary work. The point about the funding effect, and more generally about evaluating incentives and motives, is to pay extra attention to the possibility of deception when there are incentives to be biased and to lie. Incentives can be influential but they also can be ignored or resisted.

---

10 Ben Goldacre, *Bad Pharma: How Drug Companies Mislead Doctors and Harm Patients* (London: Fourth Estate, 2012).

Summary

When detecting deception it can be very useful to assess the speaker by taking notice of behavioural clues, assessing the track record of the speaker, and evaluating incentives and motives. These methods can offer signals about the likelihood of deception, but they do not prove either truth-telling or lying. What they can do is provide a guess, sometimes a good guess, about what is going on. Do you presume honesty and need good evidence for lying, or do you presume deception and need good evidence for honesty? In other words, where does the onus of proof lie? Either way, you need evidence.

The evidence

Evidence is crucial in detecting deception. The complication is that evidence can be high or low quality, and sometimes is misleading. Occasionally evidence is designed to be misleading.

An everyday example: your friend Peta says she can't come to your group's meeting this evening because she has a headache. Just after the end of the meeting, you receive a message from a different friend who saw Peta out partying. If Peta was lying about her headache as a reason not to attend the meeting, it's not a serious lie, unless her presence at the meeting was absolutely crucial, and she had promised repeatedly that she would attend no matter what.

However, the evidence that Peta was lying is pretty thin. The person who told you Peta was out partying might have mistaken someone else for Peta, or might have been lying in order to alienate you from Peta. It's also possible that Peta did have a serious headache, but it lifted later in the evening, after the meeting was over, and she felt so much better that she went partying.

The lesson here is that it's worthwhile determining the quality of the evidence and thinking of possible alternative explanations for it.

When the evidence is weak, an obvious step is to obtain better evidence. So, after the meeting, you visit Peta's home to see how she's feeling and tell her what happened. If she's there, and seems miserable, you have evidence to counter the gossip that she was out partying. If she's not there, it's more suspicious evidence but still not enough to be sure she was lying.

In many incidents such as Peta's headache, it's not possible to reach a definitive conclusion. The logical thing is to suspend judgement and seek stronger evidence on some future occasion. However, many people feel uncomfortable with uncertainty and prefer to reach a conclusion, even if it is not well supported. This might be to believe Peta and disregard the message about her partying or it might be to assume she was lying. One of the greatest challenges in detecting deception is to avoid drawing premature conclusions or, in other words, to keep an open mind about possibilities.

Detecting deception can be important for groups far beyond the question of whether Peta had a headache. It can protect the group and sometimes an entire campaign from failure by determining whether a member might be unreliable at a crucial time. The group needs strategies to keep its efforts going.

Some liars are quite skilled at twisting and changing their stories, weaving elaborate excuses and avoiding getting pinned down. If you regularly interact with Fred, who you suspect is a serial liar, it can be useful to get Fred's statements in writing, or to make recordings of conversations with him. Then when Fred contradicts himself later, you have evidence. Whether to confront Fred with the evidence is another matter. You may decide just to keep the information to yourself, in case you need it, for example to convince someone else. Or you might ask Fred about the discrepancy. He might explain away contradictions as mistakes or jokes or not really meaning what he said.

People in the public eye, whose speeches and informal comments are recorded, provide a rich lode of evidence for detecting deception. Politicians frequently give talks and interviews, and can be readily caught out in contradictions, especially if opponents are monitoring everything they say. It is no surprise that many politicians develop a way of responding to questions that avoids saying too many things directly.

A case of false credentials
In 1991, a man named John McNicol set up Whistleblowers Anonymous, the first whistleblowers organisation in Australia. I was on the mailing list for the group's newsletter and met with McNicol during a visit to Canberra, where he lived.

In 1993, John was the lead organiser of a one-day conference in Canberra put on by Whistleblowers Anonymous. Isla MacGregor and I had set up Dissent

Network Australia and, liaising with McNicol, organised a workshop for the day before the conference. On the day of the conference, everyone involved was startled to read an article in the *Canberra Times,* the respected daily newspaper for the country's capital city, titled "Campaigner coy at the sound of the whistle."[11] The article, by journalist Norman Abjorensen, exposed McNicol for having claimed credentials he did not have. Here is an extract from Abjorensen's article:

In an occasional paper circulated to journalists on whistleblower protection legislation, Mr McNicol listed after his name the letters BD, FSA (Scot), MIPRA, JP.

Asked about the BD (Bachelor of Divinity), Mr McNicol replied that it was from "an American university," and he volunteered that he had been a Baptist minister at Wimbledon in London.

When asked to name the university from which he had obtained his degree, Mr McNicol declined. Asked why he had previously indicated it was conferred by the University of London, Mr McNicol said he had never made this claim.

However, in a directory entitled *Who's Who in Australia and the Far East* published in 1989, Mr McNicol is listed, described as a journalist and public relations consultant. Under education is the entry: "Wick Academy; BD, London University, England."

An earlier publication, *Who's Who in the Commonwealth,* in which Mr McNicol is described as a journalist and publisher, lists under education: "Wick Academy, Scotland; London University."

According to a letter from the International Biographical Centre, compiler of the directories, the information was supplied by Mr McNicol.

Further, a letter from the University of London, dated November 1992, and signed by Miss U. Garmann, of the university's support services and student records, examinations division, says, "On the information given I have been unable to find any record in

---

11 Norman Abjorensen, "Campaigner coy at the sound of the whistle," *Canberra Times*, 27 March 1993, p. 3.

the name of John McNicol and so, cannot verify the award to him of a Bachelor of Divinity from the University of London." ...
 [McNicol] said the questions being put to him were "improper ... as far as my credentials are concerned, I've got nothing to hide."

The national director of Whistleblowers Anonymous, John McNicol, at yesterday's press conference.

Abjorensen undertook two tasks: detecting and exposing deception, in this case false claims about credentials. There were two elements to task 1, detection: establishing that McNicol had made a claim and finding evidence that the claim was false. Both of these are essential, because people under scrutiny often change their story. McNicol claimed he had never said he had a degree from the University of London, but Abjorensen had laid a trap, finding an entry in *Who's Who in the Commonwealth* for McNicol listing a degree from the University of London. Anticipating that McNicol might say that the information in the entry hadn't come from him — namely that someone else was responsible — Abjorensen obtained a letter from the International Biographical Centre stating that

McNicol had supplied the information.[12] What we see in Abjorensen's article is a careful process of pinning down McNicol in a lie, namely claiming credentials he did not have, and closing off escape routes that he might take.

Abjorensen's second task was exposing deception. McNicol was caught out in the worst possible manner, his lies exposed in a major daily newspaper on the day of a conference on whistleblowing he had organised. Those of us involved in organising the conference saw this as damaging to the credibility of whistleblowing. It would have been far better if we had known about McNicol's claims beforehand, though what we might have done is uncertain. Generally, if you are likely to be caught out in a lie, as McNicol was, it is better to make a full admission and apology.

However, we had no inkling about Abjorensen's allegations; McNicol was a rather elusive character. As it turned out, at a committee meeting the day after the conference, Whistleblowers Anonymous changed its name to Whistleblowers Australia and Jean Lennane was elected president. McNicol faded from the whistleblowing scene and was not involved thereafter. So perhaps Abjorensen did the group a favour, helping push out McNicol and

---

12 Various *Who's Who* volumes at the time contacted all sorts of people inviting them to supply information for an entry about themselves. The companies made money by selling the resulting volumes, at a high price, mostly to people listed in them. An entry in such volumes provided no independent evidence of the eminence of individuals with entries.

enabling a more inclusive and honest group to take the running henceforth.

As an example of detecting deception, this example leaves out some details. We don't know why Abjorensen initially suspected McNicol was not everything he claimed to be, nor why he set out to expose him at a crucial moment. Even so, Abjorensen's techniques, which can be inferred from his article, reveal the importance of obtaining documentation and authoritative support to show deception, and of thinking about possible escape routes — ways that the deceiver might argue their way out of a hole — and closing them off in advance.

A case of corruption — and lying
Corruption refers to activities such as fraud, bribery, providing special favours, and a host of other things that contravene the principles of fairness and honest operations. When speaking of corruption, most commonly people think of governments, but corruption can occur in any organisation, including corporations, churches, trade unions and charities.

Corruption nearly always involves deception at some level, to hide the unfairness from observers. In some countries, when you are stopped by traffic police, you are expected to offer a bribe to go on your way: corruption is institutionalised, so it becomes standard practice, though technically it is against the law, otherwise it shouldn't be called a bribe. But if you refuse to pay the bribe and contest the matter in court, then various overt deceptions would come to the fore.

In the Australian state of New South Wales, there is an organisation called the Independent Commission Against Corruption or ICAC. It is funded by the state government but, as its name suggests, it is independent of the government. ICAC solicits information about corruption in public administration — it does not investigate corruption in the private sector — and has extraordinary powers to collect information and compel witnesses to testify. On the other hand, it cannot prosecute individuals that it finds corrupt: that task is referred to police and the courts.

In one of its investigations, ICAC targeted activities in Wollongong City Council, the local government body covering most of the city of Wollongong.[13] The council includes a dozen elected officials called councillors and a government bureaucracy with numerous employees dealing with local concerns.

Exactly why ICAC decided to investigate Wollongong Council is not public knowledge, but certainly it received tip-offs from individuals that some improper dealings were occurring. This would not be surprising, because corruption in Australian local government bodies is commonplace. Many of the elected councillors are property developers who use their positions to influence, directly or indirectly, decisions made about local devel-

---

13 In this account, I draw on "Corruption tactics: outrage management in a local government scandal," *Resistance Studies Magazine,* 2012, http://www.bmartin.cc/pubs/12rsm.html, which provides a detailed analysis. The paragraphs referring to Frank Vellar are taken directly from this article.

opment. For example, if an area of land is rezoned from residential to commercial, this provides a windfall profit to the owner of the land. If anyone knows in advance about the rezoning, they can buy the land and benefit financially. Alternatively, the decision about which areas to rezone can be influenced by the current owners, who might bribe council staff who make the decisions. The same sort of thing can occur with approvals for buildings and other developments.

This sort of corruption thrives on secrecy and lying. No one publicly admits that rules are being broken. Corruption can occur under the noses of other staff, and often only a few individuals know about special deals.

One or more individuals reported their suspicions or evidence of corruption to ICAC, and ICAC decided to investigate further. The investigators tapped the telephones of key people in the council, including councillors and staff. After collecting quite a bit of evidence from these telephone taps, ICAC carried out a raid on the council building, confiscating paper files and computers and searching the contents for additional evidence.

Until the raid, which was public, ICAC's investigation was secret: ICAC used its own confidential processes to collect information, first from those who reported their suspicions and then in setting up the telephone taps. After the raid, ICAC took several months to analyse the information it had collected, and then ran public hearings in which witnesses were compelled to attend and answer questions. If they refused, they could be charged under the ICAC Act, with criminal penalties probably worse than what would happen to them otherwise.

At the public hearings, various people were put on the stand and asked to answer questions. The questions were usually put by Noel Hemmings, senior counsel for ICAC, and occasionally by the Commissioner himself. Some of the people questioned were the ones suspected of corruption; others were called as credible witnesses or experts concerning the matters addressed. The questioning of the individuals suspected of corruption was revealing. Hemmings prepared the ground well, seeking to pin down the individual on the stand in a lie, by obtaining admissions to close off loopholes, namely ways they could explain away evidence. Then the witness would be confronted with a recording, played immediately after their statements, of their own conversations — obtained through telephone taps — that showed that they were lying. Or so it seemed to nearly everyone in the room. Despite seemingly irrefutable evidence of lying, nearly everyone who testified refused to admit it, and gave some other explanation. This could be considered a continuation of the lying, or just as a reluctance to admit to lying.

Frank Vellar, a property developer, denied asking for approval of his development application via planner John Gilbert. In the ICAC hearings, Hemmings, asked Vellar "Had you asked Mr Gilbert to have his computer used to record the consent so that Ms Morgan's name would not appear on it?" Vellar answered "No, I did not." Hemmings, to limit Vellar's room to manoeuvre, asked "Did you have a conversation on that line?" Vellar: "No I did not."

At this point a recording was played of a conversation between Gilbert, Morgan and Vellar. Hemmings then asked, "I asked you questions as to whether you had made any application to Mr Gilbert or Mr Oxley that the application be signed by him and not Ms Morgan. Do you recall that?" Vellar: "Yes." Hemmings: "And you denied it?" Vellar: "Because I did not recollect what you had asked me." Hemmings: "You didn't recollect?" Vellar: "You had asked me, I believe a question that I did not understand correctly. By playing the tape I have heard now what you were asking me." Vellar thus avoided admitting to a lie.

The experience at the ICAC hearings reveals, in a stark fashion, people's reluctance to admit to lying. The implication is that you may be able to find good evidence that someone is lying, but getting them to accept it can be much more difficult. If your aim is to force an admission or, more realistically, to make the lying obvious to others, then you need evidence that is detailed and specific. You need to be prepared for face-saving explanations such as "That's not what I meant" or "I was just making a joke" or "That wasn't me" or "That's taken out of context" or — as in the case of Frank Vellar — "I didn't understand." At the ICAC hearings, witnesses were compelled to answer questions. In most other situations, people can avoid admitting to lying by simply refusing to comment, changing the topic or by counter-attacking, for example accusing you of lying or of bullying.

More on the evidence
For detecting deception, it is crucial to collect and evaluate evidence. Evidence on its own is not sufficient, because the evidence might be wrong, intentionally

misleading, poor quality or not relevant. Collecting and evaluating evidence sometimes can be quick and easy, such as watching for when someone leaves a house, or can be lengthy and elaborate, equivalent to a major research project. Evidence can be used to clarify key concepts, expose contradictions and conflicting claims, to verify facts and to reassess assumptions.

One useful check is to ask whether evidence from the same source has previously been reliable. Suppose one of the members of your group is in touch with an informant in the government and is telling you about plans for policy, including attempts to hide information the public will not like and to offer misleading arguments for policies that will serve special interests. On six previous occasions, the informant's information has proved accurate. This gives you some assurance that the next bit of inside information will be accurate too, though it's not a guarantee. It's possible the informant might have been setting you up with accurate information in order to mislead you on something important, or that government officials have identified the informant and are now feeding the informant misleading information.

The Big Short

The global financial crisis provides a rich source of examples about detecting deception. Many individuals and groups in the financial sector were involved in fraudulent or misleading activities. In the US, the heart of the crisis, agents in the home loan sector provided loans to individuals who had no prospect of ever paying them back. Some of these so-called subprime home loans went to people with no jobs and no income. These people were sold on a false hope of home ownership and not informed they would lose a lot of money a few years later, as well as become homeless.

Who would want to invest in a subprime mortgage? To make such loans seem attractive to investors, several mortgages were bundled together. Some of the mortgages were considered extremely likely to be repaid: these were called AAA. Others were less reliable, called AA, A, BBB, BB and B. The B types were subprime loans. The deception in bundling mortgages was to label the package of loans according to the best ones. A bundle that was half in the B category would still be labelled AAA and sold to institutional investors as highly secure. They would better be called "junk bonds," meaning they had little or no value.

Then there were bundles of subprime mortgages. These were called collateral debt obligations or CDOs and sold as if they were worth something. When loan defaults started snowballing in 2007, banks were caught holding billions of dollars worth of junk bonds. Those who knew the risk quickly sold (unloaded) these bonds — soon to become worthless — to naïve investors. It was another deception.

Then there were the rating agencies, most prominently Moody's and Standard & Poor. To maintain their business with the banks, they gave false ratings on junk bonds. This was a gross deception, equivalent to a sports referee saying a team had scored when actually they had lost the ball midfield.

Michael Lewis undertakes investigative work and writes stories that read like novels. He has taken a special interest in financial operations. One of his books, *The Big Short* — later made into an award-winning movie — is about individuals in the financial scene who figured out that the US home-loan sector was going to melt down due to all the subprime mortgages.[14] The methods used by these operators illustrate different ways of detecting deception. One qualification is necessary: in much of the financial sector, ignorance and short-sighted self-interest rather than deception can explain much of the behaviour that led to the crisis.

Michael Burry, a stock market investor, was acclaimed for his astute understanding of markets. He had an eye for numbers while remaining independent of public opinion. He scanned through prospectuses of subprime mortgage bonds and came to the conclusion that the housing mortgage market would begin to collapse in early 2007, when variable mortgage rates would become much greater, causing owners to default on their loans. Seeking to take advantage of this knowledge, he entered into mortgage swaps with banks, essentially betting that the housing boom would go bust, eventually putting over a billion dollars into this bet. Given that housing bonds were widely seen as the most stable of investments, the companies he approached for the swaps thought they were getting something for nothing at Burry's expense.

---

14 Michael Lewis, *The Big Short: Inside the Doomsday Machine* (Penguin, 2011).

A hedge fund manager, Steve Eisman, was sceptical of the investing orthodoxy. He started focusing on the lenders and borrowers. To check what was happening, his partners visited new housing estates in Miami. These were huge houses costing far more than the usual US home, yet the owners had little income. Through interviews with lenders, Eisman's partners discovered that no one was being refused a loan, no matter how lacking in jobs or income.

> Vinny and Danny [Eisman's partners] flew down to Miami, where they wandered around empty neighborhoods built with subprime loans, and saw with their own eyes how bad things were. "They'd call me and say, 'Oh my God, this is a calamity here'," recalls Eisman.[15]

Then there were two young investors, Charlie Ledley and Jamie Mai, who in a matter of four years had turned $100,000 into $30 million by a simple approach: they took into account highly unlikely events that other investors did not want to think about. They chanced on information that the property market was going to collapse. In order to make major investments (bets), they needed access to the exchanges run by the large firms, but discovered that the minimum funds for sitting at the table were $1.5 billion. So they turned to a former trader they knew who enabled them to make huge bets on a market collapse.

---

15 Ibid., p. 96.

These stories of investment analysts who anticipated the global financial crisis show several ways of detecting deception. Burry used his extraordinary capacity to see patterns in rows of numbers. Eisman investigated the housing market by having his staff talk to new homeowners and the lenders who had enabled them to buy houses. Ledley and Mai did it by following the example of others, using their intuition.[16]

Burry, Eisner, Ledley and Mai were exceptions. Most investors did not anticipate a collapse. Many were simply ignorant: they did not understand what was going on. However, many of them knew about the shaky foundations of bundled mortgages and junk bonds. It might be said they were subject to self-deception. There had not been a housing market collapse for decades, so it seemed impossible and the prospect was simply ignored or dismissed. This is especially easy when everyone else is proceeding as if there was no problem.

Self-deception is one of the greatest barriers to detecting deception by others. What it often means in practice is not searching for contrary evidence. This is well known in psychology and is called confirmation bias: people with a strong commitment to a point of view are more likely to notice evidence supporting their view and to ignore or contest contrary evidence. There is even a phenomenon, called backfire, in which exposure to contrary evidence can reinforce people's original views: in

---

16 The story is more complex than indicated by these vignettes, and other players were involved. See Lewis's book for more information.

contesting the challenging evidence, their original views are reaffirmed.[17]

Conclusion
To detect deception, there are three main approaches: assess the speaker, uncover and analyse the evidence, and assess the history and context. What methods to use depends a lot on the circumstances. Collecting and examining the evidence is usually crucial. Doing this in a fair fashion is hard for many people. A common problem is assuming that others are lying because they say things with which you disagree or think are plain wrong. However, there might be other explanations, for example that they believe what they are saying or that there is some truth in what they are trying to express.

On the other hand, some individuals regularly lie and some governments and corporations are involved in operations that involve serious ongoing deception. Studying historical examples and patterns of collusion can help in deciding whether something shady is going on.

It is important to remain aware of the possibility of self-deception, by others and yourself. Self-deception combined with people's tendency to follow the crowd can lead to collective illusions. Furthermore, experts may be just as susceptible to self-deception as anyone else, so

---

17 Brendan Nyhan and Jason Reifler, "When corrections fail: the persistence of political misperceptions," *Political Behavior*, Vol. 32, No. 2, 2010, pp. 303–330. This is different from my own concept of backfire that can result when people are outraged by an injustice.

deferring to someone who is confident and seems knowledgeable can be risky.

Detecting deception is one thing. What to do about it is another. If you've just caught your close friend in a lie — he said he was at a work meeting but actually was having drinks at a bar — confronting him with it might wreck your relationship, and you need to consider whether confronting the lie is worth jeopardising everything you share. If you demand complete truth from everyone you know, you may not end up with any friends at all! Perhaps, sometimes, it is better not to know.

Graphic adapted from http://www.wikihow.com/Care-for-a-Sick-Dog

5
Ethics and lying

Key points
- A prohibition on lying has some harmful consequences.
- More useful is seeing truth-telling as one virtue among others.
- One way to help decide when deception is warranted is to look at the criteria for effective nonviolent action.

Is lying good or bad? More generally, is deceiving people good or bad? There are several possible answers. One is that lying is always bad and therefore should be avoided at all costs. A second is that lying is usually bad and should be avoided except in exceptional circumstances. A third answer is that it depends on the circumstances.

The absolutist position, namely that lying is always bad, was endorsed by famous philosopher Immanuel Kant (1724–1804) via his idea of the categorical imperative. Kant said we should look at the implications if everyone lied all the time. The result would be a totally dysfunctional society, because no one could trust what anyone said. Therefore, according to Kant, it is imperative to avoid lying.

"A lie can be halfway round the world before the truth has got its boots on." — James Callaghan, British politician (1976)

The trouble with such an absolute position is that just a few exceptions undermine the rule. The classic example is when Nazis come to the door of your house and ask whether there are any Jews inside. You know the Nazis will kill the Jews you are harbouring, so you lie and say no. It might be wrong to lie, but in this instance it prevents a far greater wrong, killing of innocent people.

This example and others like it lead to the second answer to the question "Is lying good or bad?," namely that it usually bad and should be avoided or discouraged when possible. Ethicist Sissela Bok, in her widely cited book *Lying*,[1] says most lying is undesirable and that it would be worthwhile to implement policies and promote practices that reduce the need to lie, for example when defending a client in court or when writing a letter of recommendation if telling the full truth sinks an applicant's chances.

Mohandas Gandhi held the view that lying should be avoided whenever possible. Gandhi characterised his approach to social engagement — which involved challenging systems of oppression — as a search for the truth. One aspect of this search was complete honesty. In mounting campaigns against British rule in India, Gandhi always began by writing to his opponent spelling out his concerns and requests and saying what he and others would do should his requests not be met. For example, prior to the famous 1930 salt march challenging the British salt laws, Gandhi wrote an open letter to Lord

---

1 Sissela Bok, *Lying: Moral Choice in Public and Private Life* (Hassocks: Harvester, 1978).

Edward Irwin, the Viceroy, seeking a resolution and stating his plans.

Gandhi and his supporters knew that polite letters would not bring about significant changes in British policy, and probably not even minor concessions. The key point here is Gandhi's modelling of appropriate behaviour, which in his mind was part of a search for truth. He did not claim to know what was best but instead sought a dialogue from which truth was more likely to emerge. Gandhi tried to initiate such a dialogue by being open about his motives, goals and plans. This can be contrasted with activists who, seeing dialogue as pointless, organise surprise rallies or otherwise try to mislead authorities about who they are and what they are going to do.

Another way of understanding Gandhi's commitment to a search for truth is that he wanted his means to be compatible with his ends. If the goal, or end, is a peaceful world, then the means or methods to achieve it should also be peaceful. This leads to Gandhi's adherence to methods not involving any violence against opponents.

Applied to truth-telling, the principle of making the means reflect the ends leads to the conclusion that lies should be avoided. The goal presumably is a world in which everyone is committed to seeking the truth and in which deception is avoided, so to move towards this goal of a truthful world, every effort should be made to be totally honest along the way.

Robert Burrowes, a prominent Australian nonviolent activist and author of *The Strategy of Nonviolent Defense*, followed Gandhi's precepts. In his chapter "Planning and organizing nonviolent defense," Burrowes discusses the importance of nonviolent discipline — refusing to use physical violence in response to being physically assaulted — and recommends that activists make a pledge to a "Code of nonviolent discipline." He lists one particular code or covenant, drawn from one used by Gandhi in 1930 and one used widely in Brazil.[2] It has 14 points, including:

1. I will speak the truth.
2. I will endeavour to overcome my fear of punishment and death.
3. I will work conscientiously to purify my personal life.
4. I will treat each person with honesty, openness, caring, and respect.

Most relevant here is point #1: "I will speak the truth." He took this very seriously, always attempting to try to say what he really felt.

Gandhi: too trusting?
Gandhi's position on lying, as recommended by Burrowes, is close to Kant's view that lying should be avoided as a matter of principle, at least in relation to activist-related matters. This sounds noble, but there are many traps for an honest individual in a world filled with deception.

The salt march, conceived and led by Gandhi, stimulated Indian popular resistance to British rule like nothing

---

2 Robert J. Burrowes, *The Strategy of Nonviolent Defense: A Gandhian Approach* (Albany, NY: State University of New York Press, 1996), pp. 183–184.

before it. Participation in civil disobedience by making salt captured the national imagination. The British imprisoned tens of thousands of Indians but could not quell the challenge. But something else did: a promise. Lord Irwin, in lengthy negotiations with Gandhi, agreed that independence for India would be seriously considered at a conference in London. Gandhi, as trusting as he was truth-telling, took the British at their word, called off the salt campaign, attended the conference and came back with nothing.[3] The promise and the conference provided only an illusion of honest negotiation: independence was not really on the table. Gandhi was easily fooled by the British promises. Similarly, many activists in the years since have been taken in by promises by politicians, corporate leaders and others.

In the 1930s, the Japanese military invaded China. Then after the 1941 attack on Pearl Harbor, Japanese troops quickly conquered the Philippines, Singapore, Burma and other countries in southeast Asia, and were poised to face the British, still the rulers of India. Gandhi opposed Japanese imperialism just as he opposed British imperialism. He decided to write a letter to the Japanese people, including what he admired about Japan as well as his criticisms of Japanese war-making. What Gandhi didn't anticipate was the way his letter would be used to serve the Japanese rulers.

---

3 Thomas Weber, *On the Salt March: The Historiography of Gandhi's March to Dandi* (New Delhi: HarperCollins, 1997), p. 462. The story is more complex than the abbreviated account here.

Several newspapers published Gandhi's letter — in an edited form, reproducing the sections praising Japan but omitting criticisms of Japanese military expansionism. Gandhi scholar Thomas Weber explains what happened:

> Regardless of context, those parts of the letter which were beneficial to Japanese policy were published on the front page of the *Yomiuri* on 18 September 1942 under the heading "An Open Letter to Japan from Gandhi." Rather conveniently, it left out all sections critical of Japanese imperialism. The letter as published in *Yomiuri* is a flagrant example of misinformation. The article ended up reproducing only a carefully selected fraction of Gandhi's original letter and included sentences which did not appear in Gandhi's original at all. [...]
>
> In short, Gandhi's actual message did not reach the people of Japan. At this stage in his life, Gandhi was one of the most famous people on the planet. He was widely respected but there was no internet and the Japanese people were generally monolingual. Their information came from the Japanese press. Here they were told that Gandhi more or less supported the imperialism of Japan while he detested the imperialism of the British. With very selective quoting Gandhi was brought on side for the most un-Gandhian of causes.[4]

---

4 Thomas Weber, "101 uses for a dead mahatma: the co-option of Gandhi for non-Gandhian causes," *Gandhi Marg*, Vol. 37, No. 2, July-September 2015, pp. 387–392, quote from pp. 391–392.

This is a good example of the perils of telling the truth and being too trusting of others. Gandhi did not anticipate how his letter would be used by ruthless nationalists and unscrupulous propagandists. If he had known how his letter would be used, what should he have done according to his principle of seeking the truth? He might decline to write anything to the Japanese people, but this would be withholding his views, a type of self-censorship. Or he could have written a letter that omitted anything positive about Japan, again engaging in self-censorship. For Gandhi, it seems, there was no easy way to reconcile a total avoidance of deception and preventing his words being used to serve a goal he opposed.

Truth-telling and other virtues
Rather than adopt an absolutist prohibition on lying, an alternative is to see truth-telling as a virtue or a value that sometimes clashes with other desirable values, such as protecting life, liberty or the environment. Lots of scenarios can be imagined in which a clash of values occurs.

A man, who is known to have beaten his wife on numerous occasions, arrives looking for her. He is armed and extremely angry. Which value is your priority? To tell the truth that she is inside the house, or to protect her safety by lying?

A government security official detains you and demands the password to your online files where you have the names and contact details of activists. You know that revealing the names will make them vulnerable to arrest or surveillance. Do you provide the password? Or do you deceive the security official by giving a different password that gives access to a version of your online files without the names and contact details? In this case, not only did you deceive the official: you made advance plans for lying in this very situation.

Imagine that you work in public relations for a company, and you are asked to write a statement that covers up responsibility for a faulty product that led to the deaths of many consumers. If you write the statement, you are implicated in a falsehood. If you refuse, you may lose your job. Another option is to write the statement and then leak information about the faulty product and the company's responsibility to the media or action groups. Leaking involves lying (to your bosses), yet it can be the most effective way of getting the truth to outside audiences.

When telling the truth is treated as one value among several, and lying is treated as sometimes the right thing to do, it may seem like principles of right and wrong have flown out the window. Morality becomes dependent on circumstances. When choosing what to do, lots of things need to be considered, including the people, the circumstances and the likely consequences, including your credibility as a truth-teller.

Although saying that truth-telling is contingent on circumstances might seem to be a rejection of morality, it can also be considered to be the basis for a superior morality, one that takes into account the realities associated with deception. An absolutist position that lying is always wrong is actually a form of deception itself, because too often it is violated (covertly or otherwise) and leads to damaging consequences. For achieving a better world, a relativist position, sensitive to people and circumstances, has better prospects.

People can ask themselves questions about what is the best course of action, and examine their own behaviour to come up with principles that apply in particular circumstances. When is it wise to lie to authorities? In an action group, is it ever beneficial to lie to others in the group? If a member of the group has done something wrong, is it better to be open about it now or to keep it hidden in the hope that outsiders will never know? What about deceptions you know about occurring in other groups, on your side? What are the pros and cons of infiltrating opposition groups to collect information about harmful activities? Should we use encryption in our communications? Should we invite police to our planning meetings? Should we wear masks at rallies?[5]

Then there are questions about whether to reveal personal feelings and thoughts. Should I tell others that I'm afraid to join an action, or pretend that I'm confident? If I think the cause is hopeless, should I say so, say nothing, or join in the chorus of optimism? If I think someone might be an infiltrator, should I say this in the group, say it to a close friend, or keep quiet and collect more information?

These and other questions raise a host of delicate issues about trust, relationships, tactics and principles. Discussing such questions is worthwhile in clarifying people's ideas and coordinating plans. Strangely enough, discussing when to lie can be a process for building trust,

---

5 Several of these scenarios are discussed in the next chapter.

a trust based on a common understanding of when deception is a worthwhile option, and a trust based on understanding of differences in views about honesty and deception. Of course, any discussion of lying itself is subject to the possibility of participants being deceptive and subject to self-deception, making the complexities greater. This might be frustrating but is likely to be more useful than the illusion of always telling the truth.

Lying, the nonviolent way
Another way to assess deception is to look at the characteristics of nonviolent action — such as rallies, vigils, strikes, boycotts and sit-ins — and see whether they apply to particular instances or types of lying. Elsewhere I selected seven features of effective nonviolent action that might be transported to arenas where there is no physical violence, such as being defamed or engaging in the debate over euthanasia.[6] The seven features are nonstandard, limited harm, participation, voluntary participation, fairness, prefiguration and skilful use. It may seem strange to see whether lying can be analogous to nonviolent action, or be part of nonviolent action, but it is worthwhile looking at what this means in practice.

Standard or authorised methods of political action in countries where civil liberties are respected include writing to politicians, advertising, public meetings, elec-

---

6 Brian Martin, *Nonviolence Unbound* (Sparsnäs, Sweden: Irene Publishing, 2015). One of my case studies was verbal defence, but this involved defending against verbal abuse, without particular attention to lying.

tion campaigning and voting. Nonviolent action is defined as being different from such standard methods while not involving physical violence against opponents. So when is deception standard and nonstandard? It is standard in social conventions such as responding "Fine" to the casual enquiry "How are you today?" and in the convention in media reporting to not mention that journalists have been fed material for stories from governments, corporations, special interest groups and other "newsmakers." For deception to qualify as non-standard, it needs to be unusual or provocative. An example is the comedy team the Yes Men, who set up fake websites, impersonate corporate executives, arrange stunts and otherwise use deception and humour to challenge powerful groups.[7] In one stunt in 2015, Edward Snowden unexpectedly appeared at the Los Angeles Convention Center, having just been pardoned by the President, to huge applause from the capacity crowd — except that it was an actor and Snowden hadn't been pardoned; Snowden then spoke from Russia via a live video link.

The second feature of effective nonviolent action is limited harm, namely not causing serious pain, suffering or physical harm to anyone involved. This feature is central to the classic example of lying to the Nazis. If lying reduces or prevents harm, it is easier to justify. Lies that cause unnecessary harm are not effective tools in a campaign that benefits the world.

The third feature is participation: the more people who can join a nonviolent action, the more likely it is to be

---

7 See the Yes Lab, http://yeslab.org/.

effective. Just about anyone can participate in a rally, strike or boycott, but very few are able or willing to perch on top of a tripod or hang a banner from the side of a building. Rallies, strikes and boycotts feature prominently in mass campaigns against repressive regimes. In line with this feature, lies in which lots of people can participate are more likely to be effective as part of a campaign based on nonviolence principles. Groups of activists, when arrested, might all give their name as Mohandas Gandhi. If there is a ban on wearing the hijab, many women might wear it as a form of protest, even though they are not Muslims.

However, according to the fourth feature of effective nonviolent action, participation in deception needs to be voluntary. This rules out police, lawyers or public relations personnel lying to the public because of government instructions.

The fifth feature is fairness. Many observers think it is unfair for police to beat non-resisting protesters. However, when protesters throw bricks at police, this is likely to be seen as unfair to the police, and justify police counter-violence. Refraining from any physical violence is a good way to prevent unfairness. Applying this feature to lying requires assessing the likely response of observers. Consider a leaker of secret government information, someone like Daniel Ellsberg, Chelsea Manning or Edward Snowden. They were involved in deception, at least until their identities were exposed. The greater the crimes and abuses they expose, the more likely their deceptions will be seen as fair. Of course not everyone thinks the same way about leaking secret documents or any other action, so assessing this criterion requires determining or anticipating the reactions of a range of observers.

The sixth feature is prefiguration, which occurs when the means reflect the ends. If the goal is a world without organised violence, then nonviolent action is prefigurative whereas armed struggle is not. If the goal is a world of total honesty, then lying will never be prefigurative. However, as discussed before, it can be argued that a world of total honesty would be intolerable for most people, and hence not a desirable goal. If, instead, the goal is a world without malign lies that serve oppressive systems, then prefiguration is much easier: it just means restricting lies to those that help challenge oppressive systems.

However, there is an extra complication here. In advance, it can be difficult to know when a lie will help challenge an oppressive system: the lie might turn out to be counterproductive, and then it is too late to undo it.

The seventh and final feature of effective nonviolent action is skilful use. Rallies, strikes, boycotts and other such methods need to be well organised and carried out by people with suitable understanding, capacities and experience. This may involve training. Just as soldiers need training to be effective, so do nonviolent activists. The implication for lying on behalf of a worthy cause is that if you're going to do it, do it well. An unconvincing lie can be worse than telling a damaging truth.

The seven features of effective nonviolent action canvassed here — nonstandard, limited harm, participation, voluntary participation, fairness, prefiguration and skilful use — are not automatically relevant to lying or deception.

To see their relevance is a matter of applying them to particular cases and seeing whether they help in offering insights or making judgements about appropriateness. There is a reasonable prospect that they are likely to offer some useful guidance, without forming a rigid prescription about when and how to be deceptive. This is because nonviolent action, in its traditional areas of application — strikes, rallies, boycotts and the like — is based on principles of dignity and equality.[8]

A key aspect of the ethics of nonviolent action is not causing physical harm to others. A strike or boycott can cause economic harm, but the opponent's physical integrity is respected. Nonviolent action keeps open the possibility of dialogue. Indeed, one of the key functions of nonviolent action is to create the conditions for dialogue. The seven features of effective nonviolent action capture some of the ethical character of this approach to conflict. Therefore, applying these seven features elsewhere may include implicit ethical considerations, and this may also apply to lying.

To summarise: Kant's approach, using the categorical imperative, treats lying as always bad. A modified version of this approach treats lying as an evil to be adopted only when it serves to prevent a greater evil. A more pragmatic approach treats lying as something to be used or avoided depending on the circumstances. For activists who want guidance in tune with their principles, it can be worth

---

8 On dignity and equality as core values of nonviolence, see Todd May, *Nonviolent Resistance: A Philosophical Introduction* (Cambridge: Polity, 2015).

looking at the seven features of effective nonviolent action and seeing how they apply to issues involving deception. In the next chapter, these approaches will be applied to some typical scenarios.

"So what makes you think you'd be any good at PR?"

"Well, for starters, I'm a really good liar."

Images from http://www.vectorfree.com/modern-businessman-vectors; Dialogue adapted from a cartoon in *The Australian* Media, 27 September 2001, p. 2

6
Case studies

Key points
• Case studies of deception in activism are useful for clarifying values and strategies.
• Several criteria can be used to judge deception in activism, including participation, prefiguration, possible harm and fairness-related impacts.
• In deciding whether to use deception, no single criterion or answer will apply in all circumstances.

To better judge when activists might use deception — with each other, in relation to opponents or the public — it's useful to examine sample activities or situations. I present several here, with comments about considerations to take into account concerning deception. At the end of the chapter, I look at each of the activities from several viewpoints. There is no single answer about whether deception should be avoided, ignored or embraced. It is important to be aware of the issues.

Keeping a secret
You're in a group campaigning for a worthy cause, for example promoting peace, overcoming poverty or combatting racism. One of the group members, Rose, tells you some personal information: she once became very drunk, hit someone, was arrested and convicted of assault, and

was sentenced to community service. She asks you to keep this information secret. You need to weigh up confidentiality in relation to the group's cause.

Rose's confidential information might also have been about sexual relationships, drug addiction, gang membership, mental illness or any of a host of other topics that might cast her in a negative light. For the time being, let's assume the information does not relate to your group's cause. If your group is opposing racism and Rose was previously a member of a racist group, your response might be different.

Keeping a secret may require being deceptive. It might be that nobody asks you anything about Rose's past, but still you're not revealing something you know. Furthermore, another member, Fred, might say to you, "I heard that Rose was convicted of assault. Do you know anything about it?" To keep the secret means telling a falsehood: "I haven't heard anything like that."

Some people are no good at keeping secrets. The first thing they do is go and tell someone else, retelling the story with their own interpretations, assumptions and exaggerations. Others are cautious about who they tell: they might tell a few close friends who are not involved (and who don't know Rose), trusting them not to tell others. If you're the sort of person who tells no one at all, you're unusual. Rose has good reason to trust you.

There are all sorts of complications. Consider Fred's question about whether Rose had been convicted of assault. If Rose has told both of you, then it might seem safe to talk about it. But what if Fred is bluffing? Actually, Rose hasn't told him anything, but he heard a rumour and thought he'd check it out with you. If you suspect Fred's claim, it would be better to talk to Rose first. Maybe she's talked only to you, or maybe she's individually told a number of people.

Another complication is that Rose may not have told you everything. Maybe she's playing down how serious the incident was: actually the person she hit was seriously disabled as a result, or she wasn't drunk but actually angry, or she went to prison. On the other hand, maybe she's exaggerating what happened — it was a minor scuffle and she was asked to leave the club and never arrested or convicted — to make it sound like she's had a rough past.

There are various factors you need to consider. If Rose is a key figure in your group, perhaps a spokesperson, will opponents and journalists be interested in information about her conviction for assault? Will they use the information to discredit Rose and your group? If so, is it better to try to hide the information, or to make it public in your own way to reduce the impact, perhaps by showing that she has learned from her mistakes? Should you talk to Rose about these possibilities? Should you raise the issue, without mentioning Rose, at a meeting? "What should we do if opponents try to obtain dirt on any of us in order to discredit the group and our goals?"

If you think Rose's past is going to be a significant vulnerability to your group, maybe you should check out her story. You could, for example, look up court records. Or, if you know enough, you could talk to some of the people involved, especially the person she assaulted, and find out what they think. If you can learn something, then opponents or journalists could too, presumably. But if you start probing, perhaps Rose will hear about it and think you've violated her trust. Furthermore, if you start probing, others might hear about your enquiries and start investigating for themselves. Trying to verify Rose's story might make things a lot worse.

This example illustrates that absolutist positions — never tell a lie, or always keep a confidence — are not very helpful. There are too many complications, and a suitable course of action depends on the personalities of the people involved, the details of the information, the dynamics of the group, and the possible actions by opponents, journalists and others.

What about good news? Should you ever keep that secret? Rose has told you she's going to receive a prestigious award or she has a great new job or has decided to have a child. Let's assume, for the sake of argument, that she thinks this is good news and you do too, and you're happy for her. However, Rose asks you to keep the information secret for the time being. In fact, you promised before she told you the news.

This might be more difficult, because what's the harm in people knowing something positive? Actually, there can be harm. Rose knows about the award through a confidential source, but it's not official yet, and announcing the award to the world would offend the committee members who made the decision. Rose knows about her job offer, but her colleagues at her current job don't, and she wants to tell them in her own way. She has decided to have a child but hasn't told her partner that she's pregnant.

So it might be safer to say nothing about good news you've been asked to keep secret. As in the case of negative information, a lot depends on the circumstances. It's valuable in all circumstances to think about possible scenarios, to examine likely impacts — including whether you maintain Rose's trust — and act accordingly. If in doubt, it can be useful to talk to someone who is not involved and doesn't know Rose and lay out the situation, without names or details.

Leaking
Whistleblowing means speaking out in the public interest.[1] A typical whistleblower is an employee who sees a problem at work — for example corruption, abuse or hazards to the public — and reports it to someone in authority. Most whistleblowers initially report their concerns to their boss. If that doesn't work, they might go to higher management (the boss's boss), a governing board, outside agencies such as an ombudsman or anti-corruption body, politicians or the media.

If managers also want the problem fixed, then whistleblowing might be welcomed. However, when the problem implicates managers, they will see the whistleblower as the problem and initiate reprisals. These include ostracism (cutting off collegial interactions), spreading of rumours, petty harassment (verbal abuse; requests being ignored; inconvenient shifts being assigned), assignment

---

1 There is a large amount of writing about whistleblowing. For my perspective, see *Whistleblowing: A Practical Guide* (Sparsnäs, Sweden: Irene Publishing, 2013).

to trivial duties or to duties with high demands, open denunciations, formal reprimands, referral to psychiatrists, demotion, dismissal and blacklisting.

This is a long list of reprisals, and the impact on the whistleblower is often devastating, leading to financial loss, emotional upset and adverse impacts on relationships and health.

Whistleblowers can be ideal allies for activist groups. Consider a group campaigning against use of a chemical. A worker in the company producing the chemical might have information about its health or environmental impacts — information kept secret by the company.

Openly speaking out about problems at work has several shortcomings. One is that as soon as you speak out, reprisals begin. That is bad enough. As well, you will be denied access to information. Furthermore, managers will start a cover-up operation, hiding or destroying information that might reveal their criminality or lack of oversight. For this reason, it's usually advisable for potential whistleblowers to collect as much information as possible before speaking out.

Another option is to leak, which can also be called blowing the whistle anonymously. Rather than speaking out to the boss or an ombudsman and revealing your identity, instead you collect information and post it to a journalist or an action group. Alternatively, you may decide to reveal your identity to a journalist or activist, meeting with them and telling what you know. By leaking, you avoid reprisals and can stay on the job, collecting more information and leaking again if needed. Indeed, you can continue to be a leaker for months or years — unless you are discovered.

Being a leaker involves deception. You collect information and send it to a journalist or an activist, but you say nothing to your boss or colleagues. (You might confide with a few trusted friends and family members, but this is risky. They might not be able to keep a secret.) If your leak has an impact, there will be a news report based on it, or perhaps a message that there will be an official investigation of your unit.

If you're careful, you will have ensured that nothing you've leaked can identify you directly. You've converted word-processed documents to text files so the revealing "properties" of the documents disappear. If you've written an explanation of the documents, you've disguised your writing style. You've destroyed the stand-alone device you used to write it and used a short-term email account to send it. In these and other ways, you've hidden or disguised your actions.[2] From your point of view, you're being careful. Others may see you as being devious.

No matter how careful you are, there is a risk that a thorough investigation will identify you as a possible leaker. You may need to lie convincingly to an investigator, saying you don't know who the leaker might be, and perhaps providing some cover story for some of your

---

2 Brian Martin, "Leaking: practicalities and politics," *The Whistle* (Newsletter of Whistleblowers Australia), #81, January 2015, pp. 13–16, http://www.bmartin.cc/dissent/contacts/au_wba/whistle201501.pdf.

activities. You might even point to one or two co-workers as possible leakers if you're confident they will be cleared.

You'll also need to behave normally with your co-workers. This means that when asked about the leak, you'll need to feign surprise, cynicism, anger or whatever emotion would be most typical of you if you *weren't* the leaker. Indeed, it can be useful to imagine that actually someone else was the leaker (maybe there were two independent leaks) and respond accordingly. If you're normally an outgoing, gossipy sort of person, then you'll initiate conversations speculating about who the leaker could be and what might happen. You could even joke that some people might think you are the leaker and say, facetiously, "I wish I'd done it. Damn whoever did this before me." Basically, you need to pretend to be yourself, but in a parallel world in which you're not the leaker.

If you're a trusted employee, known for your conscientiousness and integrity, it's possible that you will be put in charge of an investigation to find the leaker. This will require of you another level of acting, as you go through the motions of trying to find the leaker. You need to make the investigation seem thorough but come up short.

If your leak is about something important, something that can thwart major corruption or save lives, the ethics of leaking are straightforward: you are lying for a good cause. Instead of speaking up immediately and thereby allowing the perpetrators to marginalise you and cover up their actions, by leaking you are most likely being far more effective.

However, there is one scenario that can cause anguish. If your bosses are ruthless, they may decide to finger some worker as the leaker and take reprisals, perhaps firing them. They picked some innocent person to make the real leaker — you! — feel guilty. You might try to leak information to show that your bosses penalised the wrong person, but they don't care. There's no easy answer to this dilemma. It's possible that you'll want to resign as soon as you've finished gathering as much information as possible.

An action group and a leaker make for a powerful combination. The action group — on the environment, financial probity, human rights, or some other cause — has the freedom to speak out, organise protests and take actions that workers could not contemplate, because they would immediately lose their jobs. However, the activists need to know what's happening inside the organisation: what plans are being made, what impact protests have had, and what strategies would be most effective. A leaker or confidential informant can provide the inside perspective that can help the action group be far more effective. The action-group-leaker combination is potent — and it requires ongoing secrecy and deception.

Planning an action
Your group is planning a protest. Should you inform the police about your plans? Should you invite the police to attend your planning meeting? Answers depend on several factors.

One factor is how safe it is to protest. If police, politicians and most members of the public think public protest is acceptable and routine, even laudable, then it may be a good idea to invite the police to attend your meeting and send them the minutes. This will build trust with the police — at least if your protest does not involve violence — and can allow you to focus on what you are protesting about, for example militarism, environmental damage or racism. If the police know what's going to happen, they are much less likely to over-react. In fact, they may become your protectors if there are counter-protesters who want to attack you.

In some circumstances public protest is very risky, with a high likelihood of arrests and beatings. If the police know what you're planning, they might arrest your leaders in advance, blockade the location of your protest, or prepare for mass arrests. In such a circumstance, being open about your plans would be disastrous, so some degree of secrecy and deception is warranted.

Perhaps you are organising a "flash mob": members of your group seem to be going their separate ways and happen to converge on a busy street in front of a bank and then take coordinated action — singing a song or displaying some placards, for example — and 30 seconds later melting into the crowd again. If police know about the flash protest in advance, they may be able to thwart it. Secrecy is essential, and so perhaps is spontaneity, with the location chosen at the last moment and coordinated by social media.

In a highly repressive situation, protest can be open if protesters are relatively safe. In Brazil in the 1960s, Chile in the 1970s, Argentina in 2001, Turkey in 2013 and elsewhere, people have banged pots and pans as a form of protest, called cacerolazo. In some of these actions, people remain in their apartments and commence banging at a designated time, thereby reducing their vulnerability to police reprisals.

In this type of action, participants are open in what they are doing. However, in some cases secrecy is needed to organise the action, namely to decide on what it would involve and how to communicate with the people. So it was wise for planners and communicators to maintain a low-profile role.

Sometimes activists believe they are under surveillance, for example with political police listening to their phone calls. To test this belief, a highly deceptive technique can be used. The activists talk to each other by phone about a protest they are planning for a particular place and time. But instead of protesting, at the nominated time they watch the location from a distance. If they see police preparing as they usually do at demonstrations, this is a good indication that someone has been listening in on the activists' phone conversations. However, if no police are present, the implications aren't clear. It might mean the activists' phones aren't being tapped. Alternatively, the police might be tapping the activists' phones but suspect the activists might be tricking them, so they are also watching the location from a distance. Another possibility is that the police may not want to bother dealing with run-of-the-mill protests, and instead save their information for a more important action. Or perhaps the police have an informant in the group who tells them what the group is doing.

Another key factor is how many people can and will join an action. The greater the participation, the safer it is to join and so the lower the level of secrecy needed. If groups believe in openness whenever possible, to reduce the level of unaccountable power associated with secrecy, then organising actions that enable wide participation may often be a preferable option.

These examples illustrate that in planning an action, the suitable level of secrecy depends a lot on a range of factors, especially the likely response of authorities to protest. Usually the more repressive the circumstances, the more secrecy is warranted.

Communicating confidentially
Activists, like other people, often want to ensure confidentiality when communicating with each other and with trusted outsiders. This is especially true when there is the possibility that governments or private investigators are using surveillance techniques to monitor conversations.

Surveillance capacities are becoming ever more formidable. It is possible, for example, to remotely install software on electronic devices to record every keystroke, or to use lasers to record the vibrations of window panes and thereby detect what people are saying inside a room. There are now mechanical insects that can be piloted into a room and used to obtain real-time video feeds to those running this "bug."

Monitoring can also occur via collection of metadata, for example electronic records of when and where a phone is used to make a call or when a credit card transaction is made. By combining metadata, an individual's location and interactions can be pinned down with remarkable precision. Using a mobile device can provide signals about a person's location; driving a car may enable collection of information about location via electronic recognition of licence numbers; surveillance cameras can provide images to place individuals at particular times and places; use of social media can provide data for analysing a person's profile and predilections.

Pervasive electronic monitoring is more common, yet there is relatively little opposition to it, in part because most people are entranced by the benefits of connectedness: they voluntarily supply information about themselves on social media and revel in the ease of electronic commerce. Most people will never come under intensive surveillance: information about them is collected but never used for any adverse purpose. However, some individuals and groups have more to worry about.

Common targets for intensive surveillance include political leaders (by foreign governments), terrorism suspects, organised crime figures, leaders of trade unions and extreme political parties, investigative journalists — and activists. Organising a protest on a sensitive topic, whether freedom of speech, animal rights, genetic engineering or economic inequality, can make a group a candidate for scrutiny. It is in this context that activists may want to safeguard their communications, for example when discussing strategy or planning actions.

One tried-and-true method is to talk face-to-face, away from all electronic devices and perhaps with some background noise to make remote monitoring difficult. When sending sensitive messages, encryption can be used to deter reading of the contents: the message may be intercepted but cannot be immediately read. Other options include using anonymous remailers (to allow sending emails so recipients cannot see who sent them), anonymous web browsers (such as Tor), pseudonyms and fake identities (for example on social media). Other possibilities are to use someone else's phone, to set up multiple identities online, and to use false names. These all involve some level of secrecy and/or deception.

There is a longstanding competition between encryption system developers and designers and those who try to decipher encrypted messages. This is a story in itself, with its own elements of secrecy and deception. There are many technical details, and new options are being developed all the time.

In places where expressing criticism of the government is seen as subversive and where penalties are severe, maintaining anonymity seems warranted both ethically and practically. In 2010 in Egypt, Wael Ghonim set up a Facebook page titled "We are all Khalid Said," after the name of a young man who was beaten to death by police. The page quickly became highly popular and was a magnet for opposition to the regime. Ghonim went to great lengths to maintain his anonymity. If his identity had been known to the Egyptian authorities, his life would have been in danger and the effectiveness of the Facebook page greatly reduced.[3]

In other circumstances, anonymity is less beneficial. If a dissident is arrested, one of the greatest sources of protection is being known to outsiders, both inside a country and internationally.

---

3 Wael Ghonim, *Revolution 2.0* (London: Fourth Estate, 2012).

Infiltrating the opposition

Being a spy is a way of gaining information. It means pretending you are part of a group — a foreign country, a corporate competitor or an opposition party — when actually you are serving a different one.

Spying has a long tradition in foreign affairs. Consider for example the US and Chinese governments: each one would like to gather secret information about the other, and one way is to have agents who infiltrate various organisations in the other country. A US spy might seek to join a government department in China, and likewise a Chinese spy might seek to join a US research agency — or they might already work in these organisations and be recruited to spy.

These days, electronic surveillance has replaced much spying, and there is not as much reliance on individual agents to gather information. If you can intercept phone conversations, it's less important to actually be there. Nevertheless, individual spying still plays a role.

Spying requires an exceptional level of deception: the spy must convince everyone in the target group of being genuine. It essentially means lying almost all the time.

As described in chapter 3, activist groups have been targets of spying, the most well known case involving the anarchist group London Greenpeace, which was infiltrated by agents paid by McDonald's, which then sued five members of the group for defamation. Helen Steel, who along with Dave Morris defended the case, was later the victim of an even more damaging type of deception. She had a relationship, lasting many years, with a man who called himself John Barker. Then, suddenly, he disappeared. It turned out that his actual name was John Dines, and he was an undercover officer working for the London Metropolitan Police. He was a married man tasked with gaining information about Steel's activities by establishing and maintaining the closest type of personal relationship.

Steel was just one of a number of activists who became victims of this sort of deception. And it was a particularly damaging experience, undermining Steel's trust in others.

Now think of this from the other side, from the point of view of the infiltrators. They are paid to collect information about groups that are criminal or dangerous, at least according to the infiltrators' employers. To do this, they pretend to be activists, pretend to be concerned about the issues and pretend to be friends with genuine activists. In some of this, no pretending is required: the infiltrators might feel a real sense of connection with activists, and even be sympathetic to their cause. But they also have another loyalty, to their employer, so they betray the activists through turning over confidential information. If they form intimate relationships with activists, even having children with them, the deception and betrayal are even more serious.

London Greenpeace was infiltrated by agents paid by McDonald's. Think now of infiltration in the opposite direction: activists infiltrating mainstream organisations, for example armies, corporations or government departments. There are differences between these two scenarios, of course. Activists would become infiltrators out of commitment to a cause, not because they are paid. Mainstream organisations have enormous resources to pay infiltrators, whereas few activist organisations have sufficient funds to pay generous salaries even to their own staff.

Imagine, then, a committed peace activist who decides to get a job with an arms manufacturing firm, or a committed environmental activist who decides to get a job with an oil company. Their plan would be to rise within the organisation, obtain inside information and feed it to their campaigning allies on the outside. This would require an exceptional level of long-term deception: as well as needing to put on a mask during working hours, it might also involve socialising after hours. Any deviation from a highly conformist corporate culture would by risky, jeopardising the possibility of advancement or even risking exposure. The more the infiltrator adapts to the organisational culture, the more revealing are the insights.

There is always a risk of "going native": inhabiting a role thoroughly and for a long period may lead to a change in beliefs. Most corporate workers are decent people who are quite sincere in their commitments, and the activist infiltrator might come to sympathise with them and lose incentive to expose what is going on. Another problem is that the information gained would not be very useful to outsiders. Unless there is major corruption, and the infiltrator has access to revealing information, there is not much to report, except for corporate culture itself. This is indeed a mystery to outsiders, but is not top secret. It's possible for activist groups to interview corporate insiders or to get to know them through social networks.

The question then arises: is infiltration by activists worthwhile in purely pragmatic terms? Anyone willing to spend months or years for a cause might achieve more by other means, such as becoming a campaigner or organiser. It might be easier to gain inside information by cultivating contacts inside organisations than trying to infiltrate them. Add to this the risk of infiltrators becoming sympathetic to the people they engage with, and it might be that infiltration is not a very effective tactic.

Indeed, it can be asked whether government and corporate infiltration into activist groups is all that effective. It can be disruptive and harmful, but does it provide information that can't be gained otherwise? One thing is sure, infiltration can be highly damaging to the people involved. In this case, deception is disastrous to relationships, and so should be contemplated only in extreme circumstances.

Wearing masks
At some demonstrations, protesters wear masks. Usually the reason is to prevent reprisals from authorities. Police may identify and arrest leaders; they may photograph crowds, attempt to identify participants and put their names on lists, subject them to additional surveillance, or arrest them. In some circumstances, being identified as a protester means the possibility of imprisonment, interrogation and torture.

Another reason for wearing masks is to encourage more people to participate. When the risk of reprisals is lower, and lots of people are involved, it feels safer to join the crowd.

Given these advantages, it might be asked, why don't protesters wear masks all the time? One reason is that by being open, protesters can more readily trust each other: they feel more confident when they are among their friends. It is easier to communicate when observing facial expressions.

When protesters wear masks, it is easier for agents of the police or security forces to infiltrate the demonstration and do things to discredit the protest, for example by shouting verbal abuse or throwing stones at shop windows or at police, thereby helping justify police action against the protesters.[4] There is also evidence that wearing a mask can have a disinhibition effect: it may make it easier to steal and be aggressive towards others. Actions seen as antisocial can discredit the protest.[5]

Wearing a mask at a demonstration is a fairly minor form of deception. It hides the identity of protesters from police, but not necessarily from other protesters, especially

---

4 Members of "black blocs," who wear black clothing and usually cover their faces, often engage in aggressive actions against police and property. Their actions can be used by police to justify repression against all protesters, including the bulk of protesters who are not violent. For a sophisticated analysis of black blocs, see Francis Dupuis-Déri, *Who's Afraid of the Black Blocs? Anarchy in Action around the World* (Toronto: Between the Lines, 2013).
5 Edward Diener, Scott C. Fraser, Arthur L. Beaman and Roger T. Kelem, "Effects of deindividuation variables on stealing among Halloween trick-or-treaters," *Journal of Personality and Social Psychology*, Vol. 33, No. 2, 1976, pp. 178–183; Robert I. Watson, Jr., "Investigation into deindividuation using a cross-cultural survey technique," *Journal of Personality and Social Psychology*, Vol. 25, No. 3, 1973, pp. 342–345.

when sticking with a group of friends who recognise each other's voices. Even so, agents provocateurs have an easier time when protesters wear masks.

So there are quite a few factors to take into account when deciding whether wearing masks is a good idea, including the level of repression and the risk of reprisals, the number of people participating and the risk of infiltration by police agents.

Setting up a radical flank

In the US environmental movement, mainstream organisations like the Sierra Club[6] primarily use methods such as lobbying and providing information: they work within the system. Then there is Earth First! It uses sabotage to oppose assaults on nature, for example pulling up survey stakes and putting sand in the petrol tanks of vehicles. (Earth First! activists take great care to avoid endangering humans.) From the point of view of the mainstream organisations, Earth First! is a "radical flank." A radical flank pursues more extreme objectives or uses more forceful methods.[7]

---

6 In recent years, the Sierra Club has taken stronger environmental stands and done more to encourage grassroots action.

7 The classic reference is Herbert H. Haines, "Black radicalization and the funding of civil rights: 1957–1970," *Social Problems*, Vol. 32, No. 1, 1984, pp. 31–43. For a recent analysis, see Eric Chenoweth and Kurt Schock, "Do contemporaneous armed challenges affect the outcomes of mass nonviolent campaigns?" *Mobilization*, Vol. 20, No. 4, 2015, pp. 427–451.

In some struggles against repressive regimes, methods of nonviolent action such as rallies, strikes and boycotts become the dominant approach. Armed resistance in such circumstances represents a radical flank.

Radical flanks can be beneficial or harmful to the cause. Sometimes the radical flank is seen as threatening to opponents, who as a result may make concessions to mainstream groups. This is called a positive radical flank effect. On the other hand, sometimes a radical flank is seen as so extreme or dangerous that it discredits the movement, turning popular opinion away. This is a negative radical flank effect. Sometimes there are combinations of positive and negative effects.

Imagine you're in a human rights activist group concerned about imprisonment of people without trial, so-called preventive detention. You decide to try to take advantage of the positive radical flank effect. You think the mainstream groups are fairly conventional: they make submissions to governments, push for law reform and issue press releases. Yet these efforts don't seem to you to have much effect: your government is still imprisoning people without trial. So your group decides to pretend to be extreme, in an attempt to make the mainstream human rights groups seem more acceptable. You say you're going to arrest a couple of leading politicians and hold them in preventive detention until the laws are changed and political prisoners are released.

You might have some reservations. Your group's announcement might end up being counterproductive: it might be a negative radical flank effect. It might lead to intense surveillance of your group and all human rights groups. It might lead to an expansion of preventive detention. For the sake of this example, set aside your reservations and assume the effect is positive: preventive detention is shown up as outrageous.

Your group made the announcement, but actually none of you ever intended to arrest politicians or hold them hostage. It was all rhetoric designed to attract attention and serve the cause. It was an elaborate lie. Was it a good idea? Can lying be worthwhile to produce a positive radical flank effect?

Your group might lose all credibility if your lie is exposed. Perhaps, after the laws are changed, you come out and say it was all pretence. Or perhaps a government agent informs on your discussions, or your phones are tapped and your deception is exposed. Does it matter?

One disadvantage is that a major deception like this can undermine the credibility of other human rights groups. On the other hand, perhaps your group will be seen as rogue operators, and people are more likely to turn to the tried and true human rights groups. That's the whole point of being a radical flank in this example.

Now imagine a different scenario. Your group wants to discredit your opponents by creating a negative radical flank effect. Your plan is to set up a fake group that supports your opponents and is so extreme that it hurts them. You're in a pro-choice group and you want to discredit opponents of abortion, so you set up a fake group that advocates maiming women who have abortions. Alternatively, you're in a pro-life group and you want to discredit pro-choice groups, so you set up a fake group that advocates assaulting pro-life protesters outside abortion clinics.

Setting up such fake groups is risky, because they might not have a negative effect: they might actually give support for your opponents. Another possibility is that the fake groups might become real groups: the existence of a fake group might attract people who think this sort of extreme action is a good idea. The result might be maiming of women who have abortions or assaults on abortion protesters, with serious harm to individuals and unpredictable wider consequences. It might even be that your fake group triggers an escalation of retaliatory violence in the struggle.

For the purposes here, the key issue is the role of deception, and setting up a fake group is definitely deceptive. The whole operation, if exposed, might backfire on your side, suggesting that everyone supporting your cause is implicated. If the deception is exposed, your attempt to create a negative radical flank effect for the opponents might instead create a negative radical flank effect for your own side. (This possibility suggests an even more devious tactic: setting up a fake group that you allow or intend to be exposed at some point so it will discredit your opponents.)

In quite a few struggles, there are fake groups, most commonly set up by industry. For example, corporations have set up groups that pretend to be community groups supporting environmental causes when actually they are funded by corporations and take anti-environmental stands. For example, according to Sourcewatch, the Center for Consumer Freedom is a front for tobacco, meat, restaurant and alcohol interests, and attacks environmentalists and others it sees as threats.[8] Fake groups like this are commonly called front groups, and when they pretend to be composed of sincere citizens the process is called astroturfing, named after the synthetic grass substitute used in indoor sporting arenas. Astroturfing is setting up fake grassroots groups.

Front groups are most commonly used by corporations and governments and involve deception to serve the interests of those with more economic and political power. Activist groups seldom use front groups, most obviously because they are the real grassroots and don't need to pretend to represent community interests. It is probably unlikely that activists would want to set up a fake group.[9] Nevertheless, the thought experiment concerning radical flanks is useful for discussing whether deception is worthwhile, in moral or pragmatic terms.

Circulating disinformation
Activists often have to deal with false and misleading information from governments, which can be designed to hide crimes, to make bad policies look good or to discredit opponents. This can be called disinformation, propaganda or in some cases information warfare. The purpose of informing and educating people is secondary; instead,

---

8 http://www.sourcewatch.org/index.php/Center_for_Consumer_Freedom

9 Umbrella organisations are sometimes set up to allow silenced groups to have a voice, but such organisations are open about their aims.

information is used, sincerely or cynically, as a tool to achieve goals. Disreputable techniques include making false claims (lying), giving a misleading impression by emphasising information that is not representative, tarnishing reputations by suggesting discrediting connections, and putting out fabricated documents that seem to come from others.

Should activists ever use disinformation techniques? They are definitely deceptive, and they are potentially harmful to others. But perhaps there are compensating benefits.[10]

Imagine that you're in an anti-racist group and you are concerned about the rise of Suyptum, a militant, outspoken organisation that is overtly racist.[11] In public actions and comments, it sometimes uses veiled threats that encourage violence against ethnic minorities, and have inspired a greater level of hate speech and violence. By changing the tone of public debate, Suyptum has encouraged mainstream politicians to pander to prejudice. The group has been receiving favourable media coverage, especially from some right-wing outlets that are giving it attention and credibility out of all proportion to its size

---

10 Robert L. Helvey, *On Strategic Nonviolent Conflict: Thinking about the Fundamentals* (Boston, MA: Albert Einstein Institution, 2004), includes a chapter on psychological operations that begins "Psychological operations (PSYOPS) is the centerpiece of a well-planned strategic nonviolent struggle" (p. 77). Helvey advocates use of propaganda to influence people's attitudes and behaviours, but only for worthwhile causes: he sees propaganda as a neutral tool. He does not explicitly recommend deceptive practices.

11 Suyptum is fictitious.

and its incoherent policies. You see the increasing popularity of Suyptum as a serious threat to the tolerance and inclusiveness that you've been promoting for years.

You've received some reports about Suyptum that suggest an unsavoury side to its activities. You are sorely tempted to do whatever is possible to undermine its credibility and disrupt its activities. Your group brainstorms some possible tactics.

You know that Suyptum's beliefs seem to be an amalgam of xenophobia, nationalism and welfare policies. You decide that you could label Suyptum a cult that promotes, indeed mandates, a strange set of beliefs. You know this is an exaggeration and that Suyptum is no more a cult than your own group, but applying the label will help discredit it. Furthermore, in labelling Suyptum a cult, you can spread rumours that anyone subscribing to Suyptum beliefs will, later on, be targeted.

You have a bit of second-hand evidence that Suyptum has been very sloppy with its finances, collecting donations but not properly accounting for expenditures. You decide to claim that Suyptum is corrupt and is fleecing the public.

A couple of Suyptum supporters are collectors of Nazi artefacts, in the spirit of thumbing their noses at political correctness. You decide to highlight the connection between Suyptum and the Nazis, suggesting that Suyptum is anti-Semitic, anti-gay and potentially murderous, even though all the main figures in Suyptum are careful to avoid any association with Nazis or other fascists.

Suyptum is organising a three-day conference, a showcase for its ideas and a venue for developing policies and plans. Several prominent individuals, not previously involved with Suyptum, have agreed to speak at the conference. One of your members tells of a plan to write letters to these speakers that seem to come from a disgruntled Suyptum member, providing damaging information about Suyptum that might discourage their attendance.

All these techniques — attributing beliefs, applying a misleading label, making allegations, highlighting negative associations and circulating damaging information — are deceptive. Using them is risky, because your techniques could be exposed, your methods seen as underhanded and your group discredited as a result. So can you get away with circulating disinformation? The larger and more powerful your group and the weaker your opponent, the more likely you can use disinformation techniques and not be held to account. That is exactly why authorities use them so often. Even so, it's possible that your opponents have skills to expose your methods, and there might be some people not involved who like to expose false claims and unfair techniques. If your methods are exposed, this might be a recruiting tool for Suyptum.

The better the reputation of your group and your cause, the more you have to lose by being associated with devious methods. Because disinformation campaigning is potentially disastrous if exposed, you may want to take steps to avoid accidentally using this form of campaigning. When you think the worst of your opponent — they are racists, after all — it is easy to assume that negative information about them is correct. So you, or some of the members of your group, are quick to attribute beliefs, apply derogatory labels and accept that damaging claims about Suyptum are true. Then, it is a short step to circulating claims or using labels in newsletters, in public statements and on social media.

All it takes for this process to occur is lack of checking. Someone tells one of your members about some gossip about Suyptum, and it is taken as the truth. The information might be true, but about a single member, or it might be misleading. Strangely enough, then, if you want to avoid circulating disinformation and be exposed for doing so, you need to be extra careful in everything you say about your opponents. This is because of the natural tendency to believe that "we" are good and "they" are bad and so to assume the worst about others. This is a type of self-deception and requires constant attention to avoid.

If you are really serious about being fair to your opponents, then ideally you can establish a connection with one or more of them and check any information that comes your way before using it. If no one in your group knows anyone in Suyptum, another option is consulting someone — perhaps a journalist or academic — who studies the issue and the groups. Yet another option is to assign someone in your group to be a devil's advocate and to take Suyptum's side, or attempt to think from Suyptum's point of view, when examining claims about Suyptum.

In summary, using disinformation techniques can be very damaging to opponents. At the same time, using them is risky because if you are exposed, your reputation may be seriously damaged. Therefore it may be worthwhile to take extra care not to inadvertently use these sorts of techniques.

Appearing conventional
Suppose you have some radical ideas. For example, you think the military should be abolished, that everyone should receive the same income, that all drugs should be legalised or that seriously disabled babies should be euthanised. Should you share your views with all your friends and workmates?

In many circumstances, it might be better to hide or moderate your views. You might have good reasons to back them up — lots of evidence and carefully considered arguments — but know that most people are not interested in this. Rather, they will make a summary judgement based purely on a gut reaction.[12] For example, they might think legalising drugs is foolish and dismiss your views without serious consideration. Furthermore, they might dismiss your views on other topics too, assuming that if you have one crazy idea, then nothing you have to say is worthy of consideration.

So, as a result, you decide to be careful about what you say, only expressing your true views with others you trust totally. And because many people love to gossip, and might exaggerate stories in the retelling, you are very careful indeed about sharing your views. In doing this, you're being deceptive. Indeed, you could be said to be

---

12 On what drives these reactions, see Jonathan Haidt, *The Righteous Mind: Why Good People Are Divided by Politics and Religion* (New York: Pantheon, 2012).

lying by omission, namely not revealing the full truth about your beliefs.

If a whole group of people behave like this, the result can be an appearance of conformity. This happens in corporations when subordinates say only what they think the boss wants to hear. The actual diversity of viewpoints is hidden, and workers may not even realise that others share their views.

There's another down side of being cautious about expressing personal viewpoints. Over time, behaviour can influence beliefs: if you never express your views, then your views might change to reflect your behaviour, so eventually you don't have those radical ideas any more, or at least not in such a well developed form.

When you defend a viewpoint, presenting evidence and rebutting counter-arguments, you may end up believing it more strongly.[13] By failing to defend your belief, the belief itself may fade.

There's a related issue concerning appearing conventional or mainstream. If you have radical ideas and campaign for radical goals, should you dress and behave correspondingly? For example, suppose you hold anarchist views, believing governments should be abolished and replaced by self-managing groups. Should you dress in the stereotype of an anarchist, perhaps wearing punk clothes, nose rings and tattoos? Should you behave according to

---

13 Brendan Nyhan and Jason Reifler, "When corrections fail: the persistence of political misperceptions," *Political Behavior*, Vol. 32, No. 2, 2010, pp. 303–330.

the stereotype of an anarchist, being loud and insulting authority figures?

An alternative is to dress and behave like others who do not share your views. You can be the well-dressed and well-spoken anarchist, looking like any other corporate executive or doctor or whatever. Some people might think this is deceptive, but only if there is some expectation to dress and behave according to stereotypes. There is no rule that people attending protests must dress like the stereotype of a protester, whatever that stereotype might be. It might be more effective to wear formal dress, or an occupational uniform, and thus confound expectations.

Not conforming to stereotypes can be effective, but is it deceptive? It might clash with people's expectations, but you aren't setting out to deceive anyone and in fact you may be offering a deeper truth: stereotypes of radicals are misleading. There is no necessary connection between beliefs, clothes and verbal styles.

There is an interesting interaction between behaviour and beliefs. People will often judge protesters according to their methods more than their beliefs. If protesters use violence, then many observers will see them as extreme, assuming their goal is to destroy society: they are extremists, indeed terrorists. It often doesn't matter that their goals are protecting the environment or stopping a war. By the same sort of inference, others may judge you more according to your dress and verbal style than by your beliefs. If you are calm and polite, your beliefs may be treated as more reasonable than if you are angry and verbally aggressive. The implication is that how you express your views may be, in some circumstances, more important than what your views actually are.[14]

Back to the original question: should you share your radical views with others? You might decide to hide your views so you can fit in better. However, there's a related question: how should you dress, speak and behave? Should you conform to stereotypes or try to confound them? Finally, if any of your choices involve deception — hiding and thus implicitly misrepresenting your views — can this deception be justified, and is it a good idea?

Other situations
There are many other situations in which activists might be deceptive for a good cause. Here are some possibilities.[15]

• Helping asylum seekers, dissidents, deserters, persecuted individuals or targets of domestic violence to hide: this might involve lying about their names, backgrounds and locations.

• Investigating military and national security operations: this might involve lying about your name and identity when making enquiries.

• Investigating human rights abuses: to gain access to countries and locations within them, it may be useful to use forged identity documents, wear disguises, create

---
14 This is called correspondence bias. See for example Nicholas Epley, *Mindwise: How We Understand what Others Think, Believe, Feel and Want* (London: Penguin, 2014), p. 142.

15 I thank Jørgen Johansen, Jason MacLeod and Dalilah Reuben-Shemia for suggesting several of these possibilities.

cover stories (which can involve others lying to verify the story), lie about relationships, and much else.
• Ploughshare actions: planning actions to damage military equipment, for example hammering missile nosecones, as a symbolic and material protest against military operations, usually requires some degree of secrecy. Ploughshare activists usually offer themselves for arrest after their actions, in the same location, so secrecy is not used to avoid accountability, but rather to enable their acts of civil disobedience.
• Being a labour organiser: in many workplaces, there are risks in trying to recruit members for trade unions or building support for an industrial action such as a strike or work-in. Organisers and workplace union delegates who are open in their activities could be fired or barred from the workplace. Furthermore, employers may be better able to counter future organising efforts.
• Humorous political stunts: some types of humour used by activists can deceive some audience members, at least part of the time.[16] For example, in Copenhagen on 22 December 1974, activists dressed as Santas took books off shop shelves and gave them to customers, saying they were free, as a protest against the commercialisation of Christmas. The Yes Men specialise in elaborate hoaxes that serve as political statements, for example announcing that the company Union Carbide took responsibility for the victims of the chemical accident at its plant in Bhopal, India, and made a huge payment in settlement.

---

16 Majken Jul Sørensen, *Humour in Political Activism: Creative Nonviolent Resistance* (Palgrave Macmillan, 2016).

• Size of a protest group: to maintain morale or deceive opponents, lies might be told about the number of people attending a rally or occupation. Jørgen Johansen tells of a civil disobedience action in Mardøla, Norway, in 1969 to block construction of a dam. Activists established a tent camp. Individuals brought and set up several tents each, most of them empty, to mislead the police and media about the number of protesters involved.

• Corruption in the movement: when members of a group are suspected of stealing money or abusing other members, a covert investigation might be undertaken.

• Detecting infiltrators: when there are suspicions about infiltrators, one way of finding out is to give misleading information to a few people and see what happens. For example, if police seem to act on the basis of the information, this might be due to infiltrators (though electronic surveillance is another possibility).

Assessing the use of deception

Each of the situations described above involves activists being deceptive in some way. You might have your own views about whether deception is essential, justified, irrelevant, risky, harmful or disastrous — or some other assessment. Here I will illustrate some ways to evaluate the use of deception according to different criteria. These ways do not provide conclusive answers, but can be helpful in thinking about deception from a variety of perspectives.

First consider the view that lying is nearly always bad: it should be avoided except in rare cases. This view derives from Kant via his categorical imperative, which involves looking at the consequences of everyone doing what you do, and if everyone is deceptive, there are big problems. This view might also be derived from Gandhi, for whom honesty was paramount.[17]

A contrasting view is the pragmatic approach. In this view, lying is accepted as something that can be beneficial or harmful. There is no universal judgement possible: each circumstance needs to be assessed on its own merits. For example, lying to a friend can be justified when in helps them or maintains a valuable relationship. Table 6.1 gives a summary judgement for each activity for Kantian and pragmatic approaches.

Some of these assessments could be contested. For example, a Gandhian might say that appearing conventional in dress and demeanour is okay if that's the way you really are, even though it deceives others about your beliefs and intentions. A pragmatist might say that setting up a fake radical flank will always be foolish. In general, though, these two approaches to deception do not provide a lot of guidance.

---

17 For a useful discussion of openness and secrecy in nonviolent struggle, see Gene Sharp, *The Politics of Nonviolent Action* (Boston: Porter Sargent, 1973), pp. 481–492. Sharp was the pioneering researcher on the pragmatic approach to nonviolent action, in contrast to Gandhi's approach founded on morals. However, Sharp reaches conclusions not all that different from Gandhi's, namely that openness is usually better than secrecy, even when facing severe repression. See also Robert Burrowes, *The Strategy of Nonviolent Defense: A Gandhian Approach* (Albany, NY: State University of New York Press, 1996), pp. 230–232.

Table 6.1 Judgements about activities involving deception from Kantian and pragmatic perspectives

Activity	Kantian approach	Pragmatic approach
Keeping a secret	No	It depends
Leaking	No	It depends
Planning an action	No	It depends
Communicating confidentially	No	It depends
Infiltrating the opposition	No	It depends
Wearing masks	No	It depends
Setting up a radical flank	No	It depends
Circulating disinformation	No	It depends
Appearing conventional	No	It depends

Another approach is to assess situations according to the features of effective nonviolent action, discussed earlier in chapter 5.[18] This doesn't immediately tell you whether deception is a good idea, but it does provide some insight that can be used in discussions, taken from a pragmatic perspective, to get beyond "It depends."

First is participation. In general, the more people who can participate in a form of social action, the better. There

---

18 Brian Martin, *Nonviolence Unbound* (Sparsnäs, Sweden: Irene Publishing, 2015).

are several reasons why participation is valuable. Importantly, greater participation means a greater likelihood of success in a campaign: rallies, if large enough, sometimes can help topple a dictator. When many different sorts of people — men and women, young and old, rich and poor, different occupations and so forth — can join in, the movement can be broader, with a greater opportunity for cross-fertilisation of ideas. Basically, the movement will be stronger when lots of people from different walks of life can join in common actions.

How does this apply to deception? The same sorts of considerations apply. If only a few people, perhaps with special skills, can participate in a form of deception, this restricts its value: there is a possibility of abuse of power and of vanguardism.

Table 6.2 Likely levels of participation in activities involving deception

Activity	Participation
Keeping a secret	Dependent on the secret
Leaking	A few leakers, many recipients
Planning an action	Those involved in planning
Communicating confidentially	Those involved in communicating
Infiltrating the opposition	Infiltrators and maybe a few others
Wearing masks	Everyone in an action who wants to

Setting up a radical flank	Those involved in the operation and a few others
Circulating disinformation	Potentially nearly everyone, including unwitting participants
Appearing conventional	Potentially nearly everyone

Some activities, like setting up a radical flank, involve just a few people whereas for others, like circulating disinformation, lots of people can join in. When participation is restricted, it's more likely the deception can be used by a small group to serve its own interests. This assumes, though, that the deception is something worth doing.

It is worth looking at methods of deception in terms of whether they are a desirable goal for a future society. For activism, the implication is that the means of achieving a goal should reflect or embody the goal itself. For example, if you want peace, then use peaceful methods to pursue it. This is sometimes called prefiguration: methods should embody, or prefigure, the goal.

In relation to deception, this raises quite a few questions, because people may differ about the desirable level and types of deception in a future society.[19] Many

---

19 A desirable future society might be less than perfect. For example, there might be serious conflicts along with mechanisms for resolving them without violence. There might continue to be activities that some people believe are damaging and should be challenged or curtailed, so leaking and wearing masks might still be needed.

might agree that ill-intentioned, harmful deception should be minimised, and likewise institutional deception, and say that benign interpersonal deception is acceptable. Then there is the question of whether people should become more aware of the prevalence of deception. These are difficult questions. In Table 6.3, one possible set of answers is given. Others will differ in their assessments. The point here is that these issues are worth discussing. Prefiguration is a criterion, but it is not definitive.

Table 6.3 One set of answers concerning whether an activity prefigures a desirable future society

Activity	Prefiguration
Keeping a secret	Possibly, dependent on the secret
Leaking	Yes, if leaking remains necessary
Planning an action	Dependent on decisions by those involved
Communicating confidentially	Dependent on decisions by those involved
Infiltrating the opposition	Not desirable
Wearing masks	Possibly if necessary
Setting up a radical flank	Not desirable
Circulating disinformation	Not desirable
Appearing conventional	Yes, if desired

Another feature of effective nonviolent action is that harm to opponents and third parties is limited. Nonviolent action, by definition, means no physical violence is used against opponents. However, methods such as strikes and boycotts can cause economic harm, and methods such as ostracism can cause psychological distress. The principle of limited harm is that actions should be designed to minimise harm to others, compatible with the goals of the action. For example, if an employer is exploiting workers or exposing the community to dangerous chemicals, a strike or boycott might cause economic or reputational harm to the employer, but this can be judged necessary to challenge the greater harm caused by the employer. On the other hand, there is no need to extend a boycott if the employer makes appropriate changes.

Table 6.4 gives one possible assessment of the harm caused by methods involving deception.

Table 6.4 Possible harm caused by using methods involving deception

Activity	Possible harm
Keeping a secret	Little or none for benign lies; dependent on the secret and individuals involved
Leaking	Exposure of confidential information; breakdown of trust
Planning an action	Little or none

Communicating confidentially	Little or none
Infiltrating the opposition	Breakdown of trust
Wearing masks	None, unless the masks are seen as threatening
Setting up a radical flank	Severe damage to campaigns if the radical flank causes harm to individuals or is counterproductive
Circulating disinformation	Damage to campaigns
Appearing conventional	None

You might want to contest some of these assessments. For example, secrecy in planning an action might break down trust built up previously through liaison with police. This suggests that the assessments are dependent on the context. Still, there are considerable differences in the possible harms involved. Leaking is a much more delicate operation because of potential harms compared to wearing masks at a rally.

Another feature worth considering is fairness: will the deception seem fair to people who know about it? Of course, if no one knows about a lie except the liar, then no one will think it's wrong. But some lies are exposed, sooner or later, and that's when the fairness criterion becomes significant. If lots of people think, "That's wrong" or "That's horrible" and turn against the people involved in the deception, this is a heavy price to pay. In the worst case, the consequences of deception are far worse than any potential benefits.

Table 6.5 lists possible assessments of the impact of a form of deception being exposed to others, including opponents and wider audiences.

Table 6.5 Impacts of activities involving deception, in relation to judgements about fairness

Activity	Fairness-related impact
Keeping a secret	Not significant except to those involved
Leaking	Depends on the scenario
Planning an action	Not significant: normal practice
Communicating confidentially	Not significant: normal practice
Infiltrating the opposition	Antagonism, especially from opponents
Wearing masks	Not significant
Setting up a radical flank	Disastrous bad publicity
Circulating disinformation	Possible bad publicity
Appearing conventional	Not significant

For several of the situations, there are few adverse consequences for exposure of deception. When activists keep secrets from each other, this usually is of no interest to anyone else. There can be serious impacts on trust between individuals, but others, if told about the keeping of secrets, will probably say "So what?" Furthermore, in some cases keeping secrets serves the goals of the group. In this situation, then, the criterion of fairness provides little leverage for a general assessment of deception.

Leaking is a complicated case. Suppose there is a leaker in a government agency providing information to an activist group that enables more effective campaigning. No one knows about the leaking except the leaker and the recipients of the leaks. If the leaking becomes known to managers, they may be upset and take various measures, for example instituting greater security measures, tracking down the identity of the leaker, or playing a double game with the activist group by circulating false information in the expectation that it will be leaked. In all these eventualities, the leaking operation is potentially jeopardised, but there are unlikely to be any public consequences.

Another possibility is that the group publicises the leaked information, for example a secret plan for a trade agreement or an internal memo about the dangers of a pharmaceutical drug. In this case, the existence of a leaker becomes public knowledge. The anonymous leaker might be condemned by some and lauded by others, largely depending on their viewpoint concerning the information being leaked.

If the leaker is exposed, what are the consequences? Will there be a backlash against your group, or will the leaker be seen as a courageous, civic-minded whistleblower? A lot depends on who the leaker is and how the leaker behaves. A leaker who comes across as principled and selfless will help your cause; one who has a shady past, seems devious or who can easily be painted as corrupt may hurt your cause. There are lots of complications. It is worth remembering that most leakers are never exposed.

If you're planning an action or a campaign and deception is involved, it can be worthwhile considering the implications. The criteria here — participation, prefiguration, possible harm and fairness — may be useful for helping to think about what is involved. However, in some circumstances these criteria may be irrelevant and other factors may be more important. The key is not the criteria but being aware of the role of deception and discussing the implications.

Conclusion
Is it a good idea to lie or otherwise deceive people? Most people make choices concerning deception based on gut reactions, often doing what others do or seem to do. In an activist group, though, this can be risky because the consequences can be harmful to the group and to the cause. Depending on the circumstances, there are risks in being too open and in being too secretive and devious.

To help minimise the risks, it is worth being aware of options and possible outcomes, and a good way to increase awareness is to discuss case studies. Discussions can be with one or two trusted friends or an entire group. There are no automatic answers. The point is to put deception and its consequences on the agenda.

Saying that lying is always wrong is unlikely to be helpful. Nor is it useful just to say, "It depends on the circumstances," because this provides little guidance. One way to evaluate situations is by using criteria such as harm, fairness, participation and prefiguration. These criteria do not on their own offer a sure guide to making good decisions. Their value is in encouraging thinking about deception from different angles, thereby fostering a richer and better informed discussion.

Finally, there is the question of what words to use. "Lying" and "deception" have negative connotations, and most people do not like to think of themselves as lying or as deceiving others. Simply applying the label may be enough to reject an option, which would be unfortunate. One way forward is to change people's attitudes towards deception and to see it in a more neutral way, as either beneficial or harmful. Another possibility is to use different words. In some cases, it's possible to refer to secrecy or, even better, to confidentiality. Wearing masks can be portrayed as protecting against reprisals. Infiltrating the opposition can be said to be collecting information about corrupt and damaging activities.

The cases here are illustrations, intended to raise issues rather than settle them. It is worthwhile thinking up your own scenarios, analysing some actual cases and discussing options. Much of the benefit comes not from finding definitive answers but from making explicit what is involved, and becoming attuned to options that can be considered when sensitive issues arise.

7
Lessons

Lying has a bad reputation, and most people don't like to think of themselves as liars. One solution is to use a restrictive definition of lying, so it only applies when telling a blatant falsehood — and even then, most instances of lying are ignored as trivial or justified as necessary. When someone asks "How are you?" and you say "Fine" even though you're feeling miserable, it's technically a lie but perhaps better classified as a convention. When you say you can't come to the party because of another engagement, when actually you can't stand the people, you're just being polite.

Setting aside definitions, most people deceive others in all sorts of ways, in the way they dress, in how they behave, in what they say and in what they don't say. Rather than ignoring deception or condemning it while engaging in it, another path is to recognise that it is common and sometimes beneficial. Calling something deception should not be the end of the story but rather the beginning of an investigation.

Activists are people who want to change the world for the better, and who do something beyond following the rules or looking after their own interests. Activists include public protesters as well as those who work within the system while seeking to change it. Activists are usually public-spirited, making sacrifices to address injustice. This makes activists sound wonderful, but activism can be turned to harmful purposes. However, that is another story.

Public-spirited activism may seem at odds with deception. If someone is serving the public good, then surely they should be honest. But if deception is an everyday practice, and sometimes beneficial, then there should not necessarily be a clash between activism and deception.

It can be hard to accept that deception can sometimes be valuable, especially when opponents might attack by saying "You're lying!" More deeply, the negative connotations of the words "lying" and "deception" are hard to overcome, making it difficult to have a sensible discussion of deception. Ironically, being honest about deception can be challenging.

The first step is to recognise that deception is commonplace. Of course it is easy to point out that others — especially authorities — are lying, as well as doing other harmful things. This is definitely worthwhile. When politicians, business executives, and mass media blatantly lie or engage in major cover-ups, exposing their deceptions and presenting the truth is crucial. It can be useful for activists to overcome their truth bias — the tendency of most people to initially believe that others are telling the truth — and to subject the actions and statements of those in power to extra scrutiny.

It is more challenging to accept that everyone routinely engages in various forms of deception. We lie! But it's not all bad: some forms of deception are beneficial. However, it would be self-serving to assume that *their* deceptions are harmful but *our* deceptions are justified.

Instead, the task should be to work out when deception is necessary or valuable and to avoid harmful lying.

With these preliminaries — which may not be possible to accomplish — the stage is set for open and honest discussions of the need for deception, and how to go about it. Should we wear masks? Should we encrypt our messages? Should we announce our plans? Should we encourage leaks? Should we infiltrate the opposition? Should we spread rumours?

Getting down to specifics can be helpful, because it avoids the misleading dichotomy between lying and telling the truth. It can be more productive to look at actions and campaigns in terms of criteria such as participation and fairness. Questions of deception need to be placed in context, as one consideration among others.

Activists have much to gain by becoming better at detecting deception by others, especially by opponents. Part of this is to practise trying to detect lies through behavioural cues, something that can be improved through practice. However, many people think they are good at detecting lies when actually they can do no better than chance, so it's probably better to acquire a realistic sense of one's own abilities, and usually this means admitting that you can't tell when someone is lying just by watching them. Far more effective is collecting evidence — documents, recordings, records of investigations — that can be used to make a case about cover-ups and lies.

Perhaps the most useful thing to learn about is the role of self-deception in human affairs. It is tempting to think or claim that someone else — a politician or another activist — is consciously trying to mislead you. However, often they have deceived themselves: they believe what they are saying, which means they are not lying. Many people start out lying and eventually start to believe their own lies. They reconstruct their memories. Self-deception has a close connection with lying, one often not fully appreciated.

Everyone is subject to self-deception. Seeing that others are deceiving themselves is one thing; it is more challenging to see it in ourselves. To accomplish goals, some self-deception can be functional: when the task is enormous, some unrealistic optimism can help to get started and continue efforts. Self-deception can also be harmful, especially when it hinders developing a realistic assessment of circumstances and personal behaviour. To overcome the traps of self-deception, it is worthwhile cultivating friends who will tell you what they really think. If you react negatively against those who try to alert you to unwelcome truths, you are missing out on valuable feedback. The same applies to groups. There is a delicate balance between maintaining illusions that build cohesion at the expense of effectiveness and being open to contrary views that can be integrated into a group's way of understanding and acting in the world.

Bibliography

Dan Ariely, *The (Honest) Truth about Dishonesty: How We Lie to Everyone — Especially Ourselves* (New York: HarperCollins, 2012)
An eye-opening and engagingly written account of fascinating findings from experiments about honesty, many by Ariely himself. According to Ariely, most people cheat in little ways and a few have no reservations about cheating in big ways. His most dispiriting finding is that most people lie to themselves about their own achievements: after they do this, they convince themselves that they haven't. The experiments to test this are highly ingenious.

F. G. Bailey, *The Prevalence of Deceit* (Ithaca, NY: Cornell University Press, 1991)
A study of truth and truths by an anthropologist, surveying various ideas about truth and commenting on the common types of lying — opportunistic and ideological — and their connection to power. This is a fascinating, thought-provoking, meandering treatment, with no obvious central message but lots of insights. Bailey introduces the idea of "basic lies" (dogma, scripture, fundamental assumptions) that masquerade as basic truths.

J. A. Barnes, *A Pack of Lies: Towards a Sociology of Lying* (Cambridge: Cambridge University Press, 1994)
A comprehensive discussion of lying, covering a range of domains (law, science, different cultures, warfare, politics, fiction, advertisements) and types of lying (including self-deception), detection and the value of lying.

Sissela Bok, *Lying: Moral Choice in Public and Private Life* (New York: Random House, 1978)
A philosophically-oriented tour of the arguments about lying, covering many familiar cases, excuses, types and responses, for example lying in a crisis, lying to liars, lying to protect clients and lying to the sick and dying. The basic thrust is that most lying is undesirable. According to Bailey, Bok makes the incorrect assumption that lies can usually be identified.

Paul Ekman, *Telling Lies: Clues to Deceit in the Marketplace, Politics, and Marriage* (New York: Norton, 1985/2009)
An accessibly written account of research on detecting lies from a liar's words, voice or body. It includes a lot of discussion of lying situations, the research Ekman has done on detecting lies, analysis of lie detectors (polygraph machines) and especially the limitations of lie catching.

Charles V. Ford, *Lies! Lies!! Lies!!! The Psychology of Deceit* (Washington, DC: American Psychiatric Press, 1996)

A straightforward, readable account of the psychology of lying and deceit, covering developmental issues, personality types, pathological lying, false memories, detecting deceit and the effects of deception. Ford highlights the pervasiveness of lying and the importance of deceit, especially self-deception, in maintaining self-esteem. He sees lying as morally neutral.

Dariusz Galasiński, *The Language of Deception: A Discourse Analytical Study* (Thousand Oaks, CA: Sage, 2000)

A sophisticated study of deception, covering a range of issues, including definitions, evasions, deception about communication and cooperating to enable misrepresentation. Galasiński analyses the way debaters misrepresent previous communication; their purpose is to represent reality in a particular way, and deception is one way to do this. Deception is normally treated as about physical or social reality; deception can also be about what people say and how they say it: it is deception about communication. People can cooperate to deceive audiences: they cooperate in order to be uncooperative.

Jon Latimer, *Deception in War* (London: John Murray, 2001)

A comprehensive account of deception in war, with lots of examples, from ancient history to twentieth century war, especially World War II. Latimer covers bluff, surveillance and counter-surveillance, tactical and strategic deception, land, sea and air cases, and guerrilla warfare.

John J. Mearsheimer, *Why Leaders Lie: The Truth about Lying in International Politics* (New York: Oxford University Press, 2011)
A short, insightful treatment of lying by government leaders, with lots of examples. Mearsheimer catalogues five main types of international lies: lying between states; fearmongering; strategic cover-ups; nationalist myths; liberal lies (concerning violations of the norms of liberal democracy).

David Nyberg, *The Varnished Truth: Truth Telling and Deceiving in Ordinary Life* (Chicago: University of Chicago Press, 1993)
A powerfully argued case that deception doesn't warrant the condemnation that it normally receives, and instead that truth-telling and deception are tools that are, and need to be, mobilised for human benefit.

Steven Poole, *Unspeak™* (London: Little, Brown, 2006)
A delightful analysis of political speech, based on examining key words and showing the ways they are associated with particular misleading meanings. "Unspeak" is defined as a "mode of speech that persuades by stealth."

W. Peter Robinson, *Deceit, Delusion and Detection* (London: Sage, 1996)
An amazingly thorough treatment of lying from a psychological perspective. Robinson includes a systematic treatment of institutional lying and the relevance of power in lying, favours a general belief in the value of truth, and treats the circumstances that affect what is considered lying.

David Shulman, *From Hire to Liar: The Role of Deception in the Workplace* (Ithaca, NY: ILR Press, 2007)
An excellent account of workplace deception, focusing on routine deceptions that are built into modes of behaviour (rather than just individual tactics).

Robert Trivers, *The Folly of Fools: The Logic of Deceit and Self-Deception in Human Life* (New York: Basic Books, 2011)
A tour-de-force treatment of self-deception from a biologist's perspective, starting with deceit among non-human animals, using evolutionary arguments and working through self-deception at a range of levels, including war, religion and social science. What is most impressive is the use of a single framework to offer insights across a whole range of areas and disciplines. Trivers writes as a scientist, presenting research findings as facts. He also provides lots of personal anecdotes, giving the treatment a refreshing honesty, especially important on the topic under examination.

Aldert Vrij, *Detecting Lies and Deceit: Pitfalls and Opportunities*, 2nd edition (Chichester, West Sussex: John Wiley & Sons, 2008)
   A comprehensive survey of methods of detecting lies, including verbal and nonverbal cues, lie detectors, behaviour analysis interviews, statement validity assessment, reality monitoring, scientific content analysis, and fMRI.

Robert L. Wolk and Arthur Henley, *The Right to Lie: A Psychological Guide to the Uses of Deceit in Everyday Life* (New York: Peter H. Wyden, 1970)
   An engaging treatment of interpersonal deceit, with the main message being that lying is often okay, and feeling guilty about it is unproductive. Wolk and Henley provide numerous case studies, giving assessments of the appropriateness of lying.

Index

1984, 43

Abbott, Tony, 69
Abjorensen, Norman, 79–82
Abu Ghraib, 27–30, 33–35
activists, 3–4, 50–51, 96–97, 114–15, 117, 119–20, 124–26, 132–33, 141–42, 154–55. *See also* case studies; Gandhi; nonviolent action; protest
Acton, Lord, 25
agents provocateurs, 128
Ariely, Dan, 158
astroturfing, 132
Australia, 69, 83. *See also* ICAC; Whistleblowers Australia
authorities, 24; deception by, 22, 24–59, 70, 155

Bailey, F. G., 158
Barnes, J. A., 159
behaviour, conventional, 116, 138
behavioural cues, 65–67
Bettelheim, Bruno, 67–68
The Big Short (Michael Lewis), 87–91
black blocs, 127n4
Bok, Sissela, 95, 159
Burrowes, Robert, 1, 96–97
Burry, Michael, 89, 91
Bush, George W., 48–49

cacerolazo, 118
Canberra Times, 79–80
case studies, 109–53
Cheney, Dick, 48–49

children, 3, 21–22, 31, 61–62
churches, 39, 53
CIA, 47
clergy, 53
codes, 7–8, 10, 97
COINTELPRO, 51
confidentiality, 110, 120
conventions, 7, 10, 56–57, 104, 137–40, 154. *See also* codes
correspondence bias, 140n14
corruption, 13, 25, 82–86, 142. *See also* leaking
courts, 20, 30–31, 38, 52, 70, 71–74. *See also* official channels
cover-up, 27–28, 35–38, 114. *See also* secrecy
Cuba, 47

deception, 6, 9–12, 101, 154–57; assessing, 103–8; by authorities, 22, 24–59, 70, 155; case studies in, 109–53; detecting, 18–19, 60–93; political, 40–43; in science, 56–58. *See also* honesty; lies; secrecy; self-deception; truth-telling
defamation, 50, 123
democracy, 21
detection, 18–19, 60–93
devaluation, 27–28, 36, 39
Dirty Politics, 41, 43
disabilities. *See* T4 programme
disinformation, 132–37. *See also* propaganda
disinhibition, 127

drug companies, 58, 74–75

Earth First!, 128
Eisman, Steve, 90–91
Ekman, Paul, 6, 9–10, 18–19, 61n1, 62n2, 65n4, 159
ethics, 94–108
euthanasia, 36. *See also* T4 programme
evidence, 76–78, 86–87. *See also* detection
exposure, 38–39, 54, 150–51

fairness, 82, 105–6, 149–51
fake groups, 130–32
flash mob, 118
Ford, Charles V., 160
front groups. *See* fake groups
funding, 75

Galasiński, Dariusz, 160
Galen, Clemens August von, 38–39
Gandhi, Mohandas, 1–2, 95–100, 143
Ghonim, Wael, 122
Gillard, Julia, 69
global financial crisis, 87–91
Grünenthal, 25–26

Hager, Nicky, 41, 43
harm, 12, 22, 24, 72, 104, 107, 112, 148–49
Hemmings, Noel, 85–86
Henley, Arthur, 163
Hitler, Adolf, 35, 37, 43
home loans, 87–91
honesty, 7, 22–23, 68–70, 95, 106, 143, 158. *See also* deception; fairness; lies; truth-telling
humour, 104, 141

ICAC (Independent Commission Against Corruption), 83–86
image management, 8–9, 45, 54, 57
incentives, 71–75
infiltration, 50–51, 123–28, 142. *See also* surveillance
intimidation, 33, 38, 40
Iraq, 5, 48–49. *See also* Abu Ghraib

Japan, 98–100
Jews, 39, 95. *See also* Nazis
just world, 32
justice, 29–31, 39, 52. *See also* courts; official channels

Kant, Immanuel, 94, 97, 107, 142–44
Key, John, 41–42

labour organisers, 141
Latimer, Jon, 160–61
law. *See* courts. *See also* official channels
lawyers, 14, 73–74. *See also* courts
leaking, 41, 101, 105, 113–17, 151–52
Ledley, Charlie, 90–91
Lewis, Michael, 89–91
lie detector, 63
lies, 5–23; by authorities, 22, 24–59; basic, 20–22, 31; definition of, 6; types of, 12–14. *See also* deception
London Greenpeace, 50, 123
Lying (Sissela Bok), 95

Mai, Jamie, 90–91
masks, 126–28
McDonald's, 50, 123
McLibel, 50
McNicol, John, 78–82
Mearsheimer, John J., 161

micro-expressions, 65
mind, 16–17, 72, 137. *See also* motives
mobilisation, 39–40
motives, 71–76

Nazis, 1–2, 35–40, 43, 95, 104, 134
New Zealand, 40–43
news, 20, 34, 40, 79, 99, 104. *See also* social media
nonstandard, 103–4
nonviolent action, 96–97, 103–8, 129, 133n10, 143n17, 148. *See also* Gandhi; protest
Northwoods, 47
nuclear weapons, 55
Nyberg, David, 161

official channels, 29–33, 37–40
openness, 143n17. *See also* honesty; secrecy
Orwell, George, 43
outrage, 26–33, 38, 40, 47, 92n17

participation, 104–5, 119–20, 126, 144–46
planning, 117–20, 141, 152
ploughshares, 141
police, 2–3, 51–53, 70, 105, 117–19, 126–27. *See also* courts; infiltration
Pollak, Richard, 67–68
polygraph, 63, 159
Poole, Steven, 161
power, 25, 46, 52, 162. *See also* authorities; official channels; outrage
pragmatic perspective, 107, 143–44
prefiguration (means reflecting ends), 3, 96, 106, 146–47

propaganda, 36, 43–49, 133n10; black, 46–48; grey, 48–49; white, 46. *See also* disinformation
protest, 55, 117–20, 126–28, 139, 142. *See also* activists
public relations, 44–45, 50, 54, 73, 101, 108

radical flanks, 128–32
recovered memory, 11
reframing, 39
reinterpretation, 28–29, 36–37
resistance, 40. *See also* activists; protest
rewards, 33
Robinson, W. Peter, 162

Saddam Hussein, 48–49
salt march, 95–98
science, 56–58
secrecy, 14–15, 27, 34–35, 54–55, 109–13, 119–20, 141, 143n17. *See also* confidentiality; cover-up
self-deception, 13, 15–18, 49, 57, 91–92, 103, 136, 156–57, 162. *See also* deception
self-presentation. *See* image management
shame, 9
Sharp, Gene, 143n17
Shulman, David, 162
skilful use, 106
Slater, Cameron, 40–43
smiling, 65–66. *See also* image management
Snowden, Edward, 104–5
social media, 8–9, 118, 121. *See also* news
sock puppets, 46

spin doctoring, 44–45. *See also* propaganda
spying, 51, 123
Stalin, 35
Steel, Helen, 50, 123–24
surveillance, 119–22. *See also* infiltration
Syria, 47–48

T4 programme, 35–40
terror management theory, 66–67
thalidomide, 25–26
tobacco companies, 44–45, 54–55, 68, 70
Tonkin Bay incident, 49
torture, 27–30, 33–35, 70
track record, 67–71
Trivers, Robert, 162. *See also* self-deception
truth bias, 59, 69–70, 155
truth-telling, 22, 56, 58, 74, 96–97, 100–3. *See also* honesty

United States, 21, 27–30, 33–35, 47–49, 51, 55, 87–90, 128.

validation, 39. *See also* devaluation
Vellar, Frank, 85–86
verballing, 52, 70. *See also* police
Vietnam, 49
Vrij, Aldert, 163

Weber, Thomas, 98–99
Whistleblowers Anonymous, 78, 81
Whistleblowers Australia, 81
whistleblowing, 81, 113–14. *See also* leaking
Wittner, Lawrence, 55
WMDs, 5–6, 48–49

Wolk, Robert L., 163
Wollongong, 83

Yes Men, 104, 141

"When telling a lie, remember to look straight ahead and avoid blinking."

Graphic adapted from
http://www.wikihow.com/Give-a-Speech-Without-Getting-Nervous

www.ingramcontent.com/pod-product-compliance
Lightning Source LLC
Chambersburg PA
CBHW060528090426

42735CB00011B/2424